Successful Financial Planners

Mentors and Masters in Equal Measure

Volume 1 (Episodes 1-25)

by
Allen Duck

Successful Financial Planners Volume 1: Mentors and Masters in Equal Measure
Copyright © 2011 by Allen Duck
http://financialplanners.50interviews.com

ISBN: 978-1-935689-18-8

Published by
50 Interviews Inc.
Colorado, USA
www.50interviews.com

All rights reserved. No part of this book may be reproduced in any form or by any electronic or mechanical means, including information storage and retrieval systems, without written permission from the author, except in the case of a reviewer, who may quote brief passages embodied in critical articles or in a review.

Trademarked names appear throughout this book. Rather than use a trademark symbol with every occurrence of a trademarked name, names are used in an editorial fashion, with no intention of infringement of the respective owner's trademark.

The information in this book is distributed on an "as is" basis, without warranty. Although every precaution has been taken in the preparation of this work, neither the author nor the publisher shall have any liability to any person or entity with respect to any loss or damage caused or alleged to be caused directly or indirectly by the information contained in this book.

Based on original *50 Interviews* concept by Brian Schwartz.

First edition. Printed in the United States of America.

I would like to dedicate this book to the profession of Financial Planning and all its practitioners. By their efforts we are able to better understand our own situation and move diligently toward our life goals, be they retirement, college funding for our kids or life's luxuries.

Introduction

Remember the old adage, "If you fail to plan, your plan will fail!" Far too often we rely on hope and good fortune to get us to our goals, yet cry foul and seem surprised when bad luck befalls us. Today the need to consider our futures and plan for retirement is no longer optional, it's essential. Add to this the desires we have for our kid's college education, a second home, or a lower mortgage, and relying on nothing but fate for financial planning is less than smart.

True Financial Planners are a distinct group of professionals, they are skilled in many disciplines, the breadth and depth of which most people would not fully understand. The art of planning is in knowing the clients situation and understanding their goals as well if not better than they do. Only by having the ability to gain these insights is a planner able to play a part in how ones future and financial model could and should be shaped. A Financial Planner can provide the insights required to create the map that confirms where someone is now, where they desire to be, and how long they wish to take to complete the journey. Investing current and future assets from a taxable and tax deferred standpoint, the availability of money for emergencies, and managing returns against risk tolerance can all be accommodated and dealt with, once you have created the plan and are committed to it.

The intent of this book was to learn from successful Financial Planners -- their history, motivations, concerns, struggles, expectations, and outlooks for themselves and their firms. I define "success" as a measure of tenure, stability, overall reward and persistent desire.

Some of my colleagues who contributed to this book are extremely successful financially and manage billions of dollars, while others make a good living from a more modest asset base. Some Planners create a smaller company with a locally focused clientele. Others build companies that offer positions and career opportunities for many people and handle greater numbers of clients. Through their service and the integral part they play in people's lives, each Financial Planner has become integrated into the fabric of the local community. They all receive more than a financial return on their investment of time, and without exception, these Planners benefit from the gratitude and heartfelt thanks of the clients they serve. All have served their clients through the good and bad markets, carefully steering them on appropriate courses toward their goals. These successful Financial Planners take pride in their care for the welfare of their clients, and that truly distinguishes them as "Trusted Advisors."

I want to extend my thanks to each of my contributor colleagues for their honesty and commitment of time to make this book a reality. The knowledge and experience they have dispensed amounts to more than 300 years of combined know-how. These Planners provided answers to questions only years of familiarity can answer, as well as advice on matters of career choice and insights regarding successful growth strategies. If you wished you had a mentor or desired to speak with a master, the wisdom of the Financial Professionals included within these pages offers opportunities for both.

-Allen

Table of Contents

Don Barton, Kensington Management 1

Larry Carroll, Carroll Financial 9

Dick Coe, Coe Financial Services, Inc. 19

Michael Curtis, Curtis Financial Services 29

Vinton Fountain, Fountain Financial Associates 37

Steve Girard, Northstar Financial Companies, Inc. 47

John Grillo, Grillo and Associates 55

Sheldon Harber, Asset Strategies, Inc. 65

Lorraine Hart, Hart Patterson Financial Services LLP 71

Lisa Heath, Financial Partners of Louisiana, LLC 79

Bryan Kelly, The Kelly Group 87

Greg Makowski, CFS Investment Advisory Services, LLC 97

Chris McGrath and Josh Schwartz,
Retirement Plan Advisors 107

Harris Nydick, CFS Investment Advisory Services, LLC 119

Henrietta Nye, Keir Educational Resources (Kier Success) ... 131

Cheryl Patterson, Hart Patterson Financial Services LLP 137

Dave Petso, Petso Financial Consultants, LLC 147

Jeff Rattiner, JR Financial Group, Inc. 155

Jim Regitz, Newport Advisory, LLC 163

Jared Roskelley, Jackson Financial Advisors 173

Darin Shebesta, Jackson Financial Advisors 181

Gerald Steffes, Steffes Financial, LTD 191

Amy Webber, Cambridge Investment Research, Inc. 197

Joel Weiner, Professional Training Services 211

Keith Wetjen, APW Wealth Advisors 219

"A profession is an occupation which is pursued largely for others and not merely for one's self. It's an occupation in which the amount of financial return is not the accepted measure of success."

-Supreme Court Judge Brandeis

"I should have been asking for referrals. I would think that was the biggest thing that would have helped us grow significantly."
           Don Barton, Kensington Management

Don has been in the financial business for 36 years. Don came out of college after studying physical education and chose to work in sales, working first for a legal publisher for a couple of years, after which he moved to the Hartford agency and then worked for seven years in the trust business. He is now, and has been, the owner of Kensington Management for 25 years, they are a boutique money management firm working with individuals and group retirement plans.

Q. So coming out of school, was this your ambition?
A. Not at all. I was a physical education major. I went on to complete 28 out of 30 credits towards my master's. I was at a teacher's master's program at Weston University and the only stipulation to enroll is that you were a teacher, and when I left teaching I couldn't go back to pick up the last two credits! I learned quickly that I couldn't afford to live on a teacher's salary. I did almost no physical education and did mostly science. So I opted out of that and moved into sales. I worked for a legal publisher for a couple years and then in 1974, another gentleman and I went to Connecticut General, the Hartford agency. We took three or four months to really survey the industry and we felt that the Hartford agency of Connecticut General had the best training program, and they did. They had a three year core work plan, core work requirement, which was every Thursday afternoon and Saturday morning for three years. That gave me the basis and also taught me some hard knocks with insurance. I had just lost a $20,000 premium to a local agency due to the "old boys

network," when I ran into headhunter and he said, "Well, what would you think of the trust business?" I said, "Tell me about it; what is it?", "It's doing a business for a trust department." "Will they give me a salary?" And the answer was yes. I had two interviews and two offers. I ended up in the trust business for seven years and ran the department for three of them.

Q. So what is your greatest motivation for staying in the business?
A. My age! I enjoy the business. I enjoy working with people, and at this point, after Kensington's 25 years, I have a commitment to a lot of people and I need to make sure that it is handed off correctly.

Q. Do you think you are unique in that regard, in the industry?
A. I think there is probably two categories: those that share my opinion and they have dealt with the clients and there's an obligation, and then there's a group that typically drive Beamers and Audis that have taken their 6 or 7% commission and moved on. I am not saying they are callous, but their motivation was to sell product and not a long-term commitment to the client. That's one of the problems with the industry, these are the ones that are being viewed as running the industry, not the committed individuals that are trying to help people long term.

Q. What do you see as the greatest challenge in meeting the client's needs and expectations?
A. Proper planning from day one. Looking at the clients that I have helped, versus the ones that I would have liked to helped but have not. I have never been able to motivate them or they have never been motivated enough. It's doing the proper ground work for that actual client. The point is that, in planning, you are viewed by the first product you sell, or the first product you try to sell. If you go in and see a life insurance need and fulfill that, you are their insurance agent,

not necessarily financial planner.

Q. When addressing a new client in the early stages of their career, what is the most important piece of advice that you think you can offer them at that stage in their lives?

A. They need a plan. It needs to be explained properly that you need to put a plan in place and all it is, is a best guesstimate at this point because you are too young, you don't know how many careers you are going to change; you think you might have an inheritance, but dad could spend 10 years in a convalescent hospital and you could lose it all. Let's look at all these factors, and then we will see if there is anything from a private standpoint or a management standpoint that we could help you with today, but I need you to commit to it. Know what you are earning and make sure you are spending less. Let's get something on paper and if you can't live with it, then two or three years from now we will revisit it and we will just say that what we started with was worthless, but let's do it again.

Q. What is the greatest challenge facing the industry?

A. I don't know...faith in the public? Trust in the public? Madoff's of the world, and yet those are the super rich. I think the ups and downs of the stock market are a challenge because people know they've got to save. Most of the people I talk to know that the stock market is the best place to save, but when they lose 30-40% in their 401(k)s as they did in 2008, what good is planning?

Q. If you had a chance to choose a different career path, would you?

A. No. My ten years at the bank were good. The bank I was with got bought. I had spent three years running a trust department where we were two and a half times larger than the bank, two of the three years we were ranked top in the state in terms of profit based on assets. That was right in an era when banks were learning that it wasn't spread income;

it was fee income, and guess what trust income is? It's fee income. We were very profitable and when I wanted leather chairs in my waiting area, we got it. It was quite a little country club. We had a fun time and I was looking at going from being the head guy to a line position at a three billion dollar trust department. So I made the decision to leave there and start here. There are a lot of things, retrospectively, that I certainly could have done to grow this much faster and bigger, but I don't have regrets. I can pay my bills.

Q. So if you were faced with a college graduate with a degree in finance, and they are looking at the great spectrum of opportunities, would you suggest that they follow a similar career path, knowing what you know now?

A. Yeah, I would. I think the issue is that if you come out of college with a finance degree and you start in the business, you are probably going to start in sales. Either that or propellerhead type job where you are doing research. If you go into the sales side of it and you are successful, there's so much more money there. If you go to work for Fidelity you can get a lot of training in a hurry and learn an awful lot about trading Euros against the Yen, but that's certainly not going to make you a planner. I look back on my career and the days of the insurance companies offering great training programs. I believe it has dried up; I don't know if they exist anymore. You would do well to find someone with a training program, but it's a solid and rewarding business.

Q. So do you think the industry is currently overly complicated and products too many or too few? How many VA structures does the industry really need?

A. There's a lot of products. Are there too many? I don't think you can ever have too many, but you can't keep up with them. You've got to find a way to decide on what the best products are today because it's going to change. There are too many insurance companies coming out with new products every month. To be a positive, viable planning company, you are going to have to find the best ones and do your due diligence.

Q. Look at the current economy, also the years 2007 through 2009, and look at a new investor, established investor, somebody in their mid 40's, and a retiree. How significant is the economy that we live in today to each of those individuals, both the good and bad?

A. It's critical. If you were getting ready to retire and lost 50 or 60% in your retirement base, which a lot of people did, and you were 63, you are not retiring at 65; you are working until 75. So the economy is critical. You really have to balance risk with your goals and your investments.

If you don't have enough money to retire and you want to retire, you have to take a lot of risk and you've got to understand that. On the investment side, I think there are ways to control risk, but the economy is critical. If it's not there, you can't retire. I would think that a person out of college, about 25 years old with a good profession could be aggressive, but with that they need to be diversified. The more volatile the market gets, the more it gives you if you can avoid the major down-drafts.

For somebody who was middle-aged and had been beat up pretty bad in the last five years, my first suggestion would be to get a new money manager. I don't know how you can retire at 65 if your money is only invested at 2 or 3%. I think you need a good strategy and steady as she goes. You go back to the market, which you should have done in March of '09. But again, if you got beat up with 40, 50, 60% losses, you need a new money manager. I look back and my experience in the market for 30 years and then I look at the charts. There are

> *"I think the issue is that if you come out of college with a finance degree and you start in the business, you are probably going to start in sales."*

many times in the market in a 14 month period that gave you 50, 60, 70% gains. How do you say that you shouldn't have been there? Now if you lost 60%, 60% doesn't get back to whole, it doesn't get close to getting back to whole, but you shouldn't have lost 60%.

> *"The hit and run product salesman needs to be put out of business."*

Q. So given your expertise, and if you had a specialization it would be in money management, what is your predominant portfolio strategy?

A. Absolutely. MPT? I think that's very critical. Diversification, active and by active I don't mean daily trading; active is actively watching the market to avoid pitfalls and make every effort to be in sectors or the right capitalization type stocks or some place around the world when an opportunity is developing and then avoiding losses. But in our portfolios, if a person is willing to take our risk analysis test and assume the market risk, we will create a portfolio together targeting 90% risk of the market with an outperform 4 or 5 so you are getting another 5 or 6% over what the market gives you. It's a pretty good, conservative way to go.

Q. Knowing what you know now, what would you do differently in terms of marketing the firm, looking back?

A. I would have asked for referrals. I would have sat with my best clients more often, showed them what we were doing, show them the benefit of what we are giving them, instead of sitting here saying, "Well, you were up 18% last year and the market was up 12%." They know that. I should have been hitting them on the side of the head with, "6% better than the market!" I should have been asking for referrals. I would think that was the biggest thing that would have helped us grow significantly.

Q. When you look back to the first three years, how tough was it to sort of carve out a niche for yourself as a business owner?

A. It was difficult. A lot of cold calls. I tried to go back to some bank clients. I remember the first client and it was the brother of a local good sized corporation, private. I think their sales were about $100M a year, so it was a pretty good size and he said, "Let me talk to my brother who is the president about giving you some money." We had lunch at the Farmington Country Club and he agreed to give us $300,000. He said, "How much do you manage?" And my response was, "What are you planning on giving me?" He said, "I am going to kill you if you lose my money!" But it was hard.

Q. So you talk to people about their retirement, but what is your personal view of retirement? How do you qualify it in your own mind?

A. Probably having assets of 120% of what you think you need, keeping them invested properly. In terms of dollars. Personally, I want to phase out. Could I walk out, maybe, but I think I am going to have the desire to keep my toe in the water, keep my mind active. Although, I certainly want a lifestyle that is as good or better than what I have now.

Q. What is your expectation of the firm when you leave?

A. It would please me greatly if it doubled in size in a year and doubled in size again in two years. It's not from an ego standpoint, it's just that I know if Kensington Management is growing under any name, the types of promises that I have made to clients are being fulfilled. It's just the commitment.

Q. Let's say Mr. Madoff was sitting in a chair next to me right now, what would you tell him?

A. I would go on the assumption that he started a very legitimate business, and I would want to know what went wrong. Something went wrong and I don't think it was greed. I think he probably made commitments to people of, "I can get you 8 to 10% a year," and the wheels came off. The wheels got loose somewhere and at some point he had to say, "Well, we are going to give them that and I will make it up next year."

Q. Lastly, if there was one thing you could change in the industry, what would it be?
A. To raise the standards for planners and salesman. The hit and run product salesman needs to be put out of business.

Q. Do you have any last comments to potential planners, people considering this as a career path?
A. Just that to consider the dedication that it is going to take. It's a lot of hard work. I think the industry has to build a better income model for the planner so that it's not big, upfront payments. It also allows the planner to know that he is going to be able to make some money at some point if he can keep that 25 or 30-year old, young married guy, on track with a plan. He will make some money, but he's not going to make a lot right now from that guy, and that guy is being ignored.

"Great marketers who are average planners do much better in this business than great planners who are average marketers."

Larry Carroll, Carroll Financial

Larry Carroll has a long history in the financial planning business with 30 years under his belt, and he spent two years prior to his move into planning as a CPA. Larry founded his company in 1980 when financial planning was still a young conceptual profession. They are based in Charlotte, North Carolina. His company has 3 partners and 36 employees, of which 12 are active planners. The company currently manages about $1.3 billion in assets, offering holistic planning services to its clients, but with a bias toward investment management and retirement income planning.

Q. Was it your ambition to be a financial planner?
A. No, especially because when I was a kid, the profession didn't exist. But I always wanted to be in business for myself. I was good at math and accounting came naturally to me, so I was an accounting major in college. I went to the University of Tennessee to get an MBA. I passed the CPA while I was in graduate school, so it made sense to get some experience and put the initials after my name. That really helped as a differentiating factor very early in my career.

One of the keys to my transition was a result of my wife going to work for a guy named Kemp Fain. Kemp was in the first class of financial planners. He ended up as president and chairman of the CFP Institute and is a real icon in the business. My wife would come home at night and tell me about things that Kemp was doing and how he was doing it. It was very intriguing to me. It sounded more interesting than what

I was doing in accounting. I got to thinking more and more about it and knew there wasn't a real planner in Charlotte, so I got in the car and drove to Knoxville to have lunch with Kemp. I told him, "Look, I am thinking about doing this," and he was very encouraging. He was a mentor to me and a lot of people in this business. I broke out and started doing it, and haven't looked back since.

Q. What keeps you motivated? You have been doing this for a number of years – I've got to believe you enjoy what you do – but how would you quantify your motivations?

A. A lot of it is just enjoying going to work every day. This business is a great combination of using the right side of your brain in terms of working with people and communication, and the analytical left side of your brain. It's a great fit for people who have a balance between the two as opposed to being off the scale in one direction or the other. It meets so many of my interaction and emotional needs. It's a great mission to feel like you help people. It's psychologically rewarding, particularly when you can see yourself making a difference in people's lives.

Q. What do you see as the greatest challenge in meeting your client needs?

A. Education and communication. There are a lot of human traits that work against good planning; emotional reactions, lack of decision making ability, lack of knowledge of markets, not having a planning or goal orientation. There's nothing magical about our business, it is good blocking and tackling. You just have to stay after things, stay in front of your people, keep working on it, know what their prejudices, interests and skills are, and work hard to get

> *"To me, retirement is about having the flexibility to work when you want, and not to do the things you don't want to do."*

them where they need to be.

Q. If somebody comes to you in the early stages of a career, they are qualified, and obviously have a personal plan that takes them into the future, what's the most important piece of advice that you can give them?

A. The one thing you should tell people, especially early in life is, no matter what stage of life you are in, spend less than you make. If you do that, so many other things will take care of themselves. For part B, you need to manage your debt wisely. Don't be over leveraged and do not use debt for consumption. That sets the stage for long term success from a financial perspective. When you get out of the financial side, again it's trite, but I have told a number of my clients: "Life is too short to not get up and enjoy going to work". Find something you are good at. If you are good at it, you'll like it, and if you don't like going to work, look for something that you want to do. I know it's simple, but I really think that this is an important long-term idea. I did a radio show in Charlotte for about four years in the mid-90s, and now once or twice a year they invite me back to do some Q&A and updates on the economy and the markets. In terms of growing my practice, it's easily the best thing I ever did.

Q. What do you see as the greatest challenge facing the industry?

A. It sounds pretty negative, but we are in a market of low returns, maybe no returns, over the next five to ten years. Only 3% of baby boomers are prepared for retirement, which means 97% are not. This is a huge challenge for us, not only to help those people, but to bring realism to their situation so they see that this may not be the retirement they planned on. "You are probably not going to get to walk out at 62. You have a lot of work to do." It's a good challenge. It means there's going to be a good bit of business out there, but I continue to see many do not have a realistic view of what their retirement is going to look like.

Q. So in terms of the hierarchy of the industry as a whole, what frustrates you the most?

A. Probably pure product people, working under the guise of financial planners. The public has great difficulty differentiating whether it's an independent planner or insurance or the Merrill-Lynch rep. We have been trying to overcome that for almost as long as I have been in the business, but it was easier to differentiate before every broker and insurance agent decided to call themselves a financial planner. It's an ongoing challenge, and when the client gets bad advice I don't think they can easily understand why.

Q. If a college graduate walks in your office with a degree in finance as opposed to being a graduate of the CFP School, what would your advice be to them?

A. Most of them don't want to hear the first step, but I tell them to go work for a big company first. It adds credibility to your resume. A lot of college graduates need the structure and the training that comes with a big company environment early in their career, and if you want to be a financial advisor, nobody is giving their money to a 23 year old anyway. You need to get some good experience, add to your skill level and mature a little bit before you look at transitioning into this business. I am a big believer in the independent model. I enjoy the flexibility I get from being independent. There's enough back-office structure out there, but nothing you can't do as an independent at this point. The last thing I always tell them is this is the best business in the world once you get to critical mass, but very difficult business before that. Going from zero to having a practice that covers all your overhead and provides you some income is a difficult process, but once you get there and can start adding to that, it's great in terms of the work, the mission of helping people, the compensation, and the flexibility you get in your work schedule. It's got it all!

Q. Do you feel the industry today is overly complicated in the products – too few or maybe too many?

A. There are too many redundant products. I can't imagine the world needs another large, cap-core mutual fund. There are too many products, or too much time and effort spent on returns and not enough products or emphasis on goals. If I bought you a good, solid, large, cap-core fund and it beat the S & P by 1% a year consistently, it would be performing well. If that 1% still gets you a zero return and you miss all your goals, it doesn't matter. We spend all this time and effort on beating indexes, when the business needs to be much more focused on goals. What are we trying to accomplish? There needs to be a focus on products accomplishing specific goals, and I think there will be over time. There's more and more effort being spent on the idea of almost annuity-like mutual funds. We will evolve there but it sure is going slowly.

> "It's interesting to point out that modern portfolio theory was first introduced in 1952, which happens to be the year I was born."

Q. If there was one product that you could create without fear of regulatory intervention, what would it be?

A. It would probably be a guaranteed income approach without all the fees that come with a VA.

Q. Given our current economy, and by that I mean the last two or three years, how significant do you think this is relative to someone who is new to investing in the early stages of their career, versus somebody who is in their aggregation phase of their mid 40's early 50's, versus somebody who is already retired?

A. With younger people it leads to a lack of confidence in the saving and accumulation process. I have had children of my existing clients decide that they want to stop making contributions to their 401K because it's not making any money. It impacts them, but I am more concerned about the psychological impact of it and them making bad decisions than I am about the true economic impact of it.

One of the really big issues in the middle-aged and retired group is the combination of lower returns from stocks and bonds. These clients realize how much risk they have in the bond market at this point, but the combination of what's going on in the stock market, the bond market and what's going on in the real estate market. Real estate prices are going back to where they were three or four years ago within the next 10 or 15 years and its confusing to a lot of people. The psychology of real estate has changed significantly. It particularly affects people who were planning to sell their home at retirement and downsize. They are looking forward to all that capital but it is not there anymore or certainly not as much as before. The concept of real estate is in the process of changing fairly significantly. I don't know about where you were, but we are in a good area that has had a pretty steady economy and people tended to buy as much house as they could. They looked at it as a savings vehicle plus there was some status involved. The people who, four years ago were candidates to buy a million dollar house, that million dollar house now sells for $700,000, but that person is perfectly content buying a $500,000 house instead. He doesn't feel like he needs or should move up and try to stretch and get the million dollar house. That's why there's an awful lot to be worked through in real estate markets that's going to affect a whole lot of that middle and retired group.

> "...it was easier to differentiate before every broker and insurance agent decided to call themselves a financial planner."

Q. Do you operate a particular portfolio strategy and has that changed in the last three years?
A. It has not changed. We are active managers and very tactical in what we do. We are looking for things that we think

are undervalued. We are looking for – for lack of a better term – regression to the main types of situations where certain areas or certain industries are cheap for some reason. We are very risk-oriented in our decision making process on the modern portfolio theory. It's interesting to point out that modern portfolio theory was first introduced in 1952, which happens to be the year I was born. I am an old man now. So there's not a lot that's modern about modern portfolio theory, in my mind.

Q. Today would you consider running your company an equal challenge to managing clients, or have you structured it in such a manner that you actually have dedicated managers to allow you to do what you always wanted to do?
A. I have dedicated managers but I do manage the company. I had an MBA before I got into this and I worked for, what was then, one of the big accounting firms. To me, managing the company is pretty easy because of my good health and because I feel like I control things on that side. I make decisions and I get things done on an as-needed basis. I find managing the clients and trying to meet their needs much more of a challenge.

Q. What does your average work week look like at this juncture?
A. When I'm in town and working, I still work nine to ten hour days, but a typical work week is probably three and a half to four days. I play golf once or twice, or go to the mountains on Thursday nights to a second home. So I still work hard when I am at work, but I am just not there quite as much. I also take four to five weeks of vacation each year.

Q. At what point in your career of 30 years, did extended time away from the office start to increase?
A. One of the big factors was adding my son to my practice. He has an MBA with an M.A. in financial mathematics from the University of Chicago. He's a CFA, and there's just nothing here that I cannot easily pass on to him. It doesn't have to be

your son, but you really need an infrastructure and support to get out like that. It doesn't do me any good to leave here and go to the mountains if I have to stay on my computer the whole time answering emails and dealing with work issues.

Q. So you mentioned your radio show as being the most successful marketing strategy you ever employed. Did you stumble onto that or was that a strategic move on your part?

A. I was at one time in the early to mid-80s, the president of the FPA, probably still the youngest president that they have ever had. We did a press release when I was named the chairmen-elect, and a local radio personality saw the press release in the paper and called and asked if I would come on the show. I said, "Yeah, I'd love to." I went in and we talked about planning and different things, took a few phone calls, it went great, and then he asked if I would be willing to come back maybe quarterly. I agreed. I went back and probably a year and a half later, they hired a brand new general manager. He heard the program and then called me the next morning. He asked if I would do a weekly program, so there was no forethought to it at all. I said yes and it turned out to be the best thing I ever did.

> *"This business is a great combination of using the right side of your brain in terms of working with people and communication, and the analytical left side of your brain."*

There was someone else hosting it. That's a great way to do it because they introduce you and build you up. They say things that you couldn't comfortably say about yourself. They control the flow of the conversation and the phone calls, and it's much better than just being there alone. Four years later they wanted to move me to the weekends, and I turned it down. I told them I already work Monday through Friday and I'm not going to work Saturday or Sundays too. If you do that it just becomes a second job, so we parted ways at that point. But if I was given the opportunity to do it again and do an hour on a regular day with a host, I would tomorrow.

Q. How tough were the first three years for you as a planner?
A. Well, if you didn't need any income it really wasn't all that bad! I was fortunate my wife was already working for Merrill-Lynch at that point. She basically supported us for the first three years or so. I don't look back and say it was easy, but I did cover my overhead pretty quickly, it's just that I wasn't making any profit. We were both confident that this would end up being good. I didn't know it would be this good, but I knew it would work over time. I believed in it.

Q. What is your personal view of your retirement?
A. I just don't see myself walking out of here. I enjoy it too much. To me, retirement is about having the flexibility to work when you want, and not to do the things you don't want to do. If you can get those two goals accomplished, that qualifies as retirement.

Q. In a worst case scenario, which one of your partners would succeed you?
A. Good question. My son would take my practice in terms of my clients. The other partners, and one partner in particular, would take over as managing partner of the firm.

Q. My favorite character of the last three years, in a jaundice sense of course, is Bernie Madoff. The question is, how detrimental was his impact on our industry?
A. Our community didn't have much exposure to him. I can't imagine you can get a straight answer, but I would love to ask the guy, "What were you thinking?" It was inevitable that he would get caught! It's just an amazing thing to me. I suspect in South Florida and New York and a couple other communities there is more lingering effect than there is in Charlotte, North Carolina.

Q. If there was one thing you could change in the industry what would it be?

A. There are minor things on the regulatory side, for example, I hope for a better understanding by clients of what we do versus what a stockbroker does or an insurance agent. I have seen this business come a long way in the past 30 years, and I think we will continue to evolve in a good direction. We are doing a lot of the right things. I think we will be rewarded for it over time.

Q. Any last comment or observation or suggestion you wanted to add?

A. I wrote down one other point that people early in their career need to understand, particularly if they are moving into this business, and in some cases for fairly ideological reasons. The point I make is great marketers who are average planners do much better in this business than great planners who are average marketers.

"Even the days that are sometimes frustrating for me in the overall scheme of things, have been pretty good days."
Dick Coe, Coe Financial Services, Inc.

Dick Coe has been a certified financial planner for 27 years. He worked in life insurance and securities for two years before getting his CFP designation. Combined, he has a total of 29 years of professional experience in the business. Dick came from a banking background working with Continental Bank, then Chicago's largest commercial bank. Dick currently has about 120 clients with fee-based assets under management of a little over $70 million. He also does some direct business, roughly speaking about $30 million. Dick has a total of four people in his firm who provide financial planning and asset management. The majority of his clients are approaching retirement, or have already retired.

Q. Was a career in financial planning a childhood ambition?
A. I had an interest in the stock market at an early age. I started buying stocks with paper route dollars, shoveling snow money, and lawn mowing money, all while literally in junior high. The term "financial planning" was not used when I was growing up. The first time I heard the term was from a CPA friend in Chicago in about 1978, he told me there was a new field emerging and he said, "Dick, you'd be great at it." I was an economics major in college, and right out of college I got my MBA in finance and accounting. My preparatory years of education and early career helped to pave the way for my career.

Q. What is your greatest motivation for continuing to be a financial planner?
A. I enjoy and appreciate the opportunity to help people while

helping myself, with a great deal of flexibility in how I manage the business, my discretionary time, etc. I enjoy the variety of the business, and I thoroughly enjoy learning not only about investments and the economy, but about a variety of personal financial planning matters. Whether it is estate planning, tax issues, retirement issues, or insurance issues, there's always been so much to learn with lots of potential for both breadth and depth of learning.

Q. What do you see as being your greatest challenge in meeting your client's needs and expectations?

A. The gratification and spending deferral have become more and more of an issue over time. People get used to a certain lifestyle and sometimes think that at retirement they can reduce it dramatically. I think there's a little naivety in that. It can be more difficult to adjust downward than some might expect. Most of our clients are long-term clients. Some have been with us since 1983. We have very high client retention. We have always done a fair amount of education through some combination of review sessions, client newsletters, seminars, etc. As far as how receptive our clients are to these methods, we have a high level of consistency with regard to review sessions. I really don't know how closely our clients read our newsletters. When I write letters to them on the economy, which I have done on a number of occasions in the last year or two – I think those letters get read. When we offer educational seminars it's mixed. Most of our clients do not attend the educational seminars, but typically enough to make a respectable turnout.

> *"People get used to a certain lifestyle and sometimes think that at retirement they can reduce it dramatically."*

Q. When addressing a new client in the early stages of their career, what is the single most important piece of advice that you give them?

A. If they are in the early stages of their career, we recommend systematic investing and a long-term approach, willingness to live with the ups and downs of the market, etc. Live with the bounces.

Q. What is the greatest challenge facing our industry?
A. The regulatory environment and the natural inclination for a certain degree of paranoia because of that regulatory climate. There's an incredible amount of pettiness in the regulatory world. The regulators prefer to focus on, almost meaningless, petty issues rather than consumer protection and avoiding frauds, such as Madoff.

Q. What would you qualify as your greatest frustration in terms of your position in the industry and maintaining that position in the industry?
A. Just to give you an example, we have a very clean record and a month ago we had a surprise audit by the Office of the Kansas Securities Commissioner one morning. I already had a client in the office meeting with an associate and expecting to see me. They asked, "What does your day look like?" I was at the front desk looking at the calendar with the office manager and said, "Actually, it's an unusually busy day. It looks like we have about five appointments. I think tomorrow would be much better. Let's look at that." We looked at that and I said, "Tomorrow is really open and it would be much easier for me to have time with you tomorrow."

I was told, "Well, I will just go ahead and get started some place and when you are out of the first meeting we will talk." So that's how it started. Then, when we actually met, he said, "You know, we are familiar with your operation so I will only be two or three hours today. With other places we would be here for two to three days." Then he said, "I will send you an email either later today or tomorrow with a request." I expected it to be short and sweet, but the next day I got a five page letter with 39 different items, many of which were multiple requests. If he had just taken the time to read all the things we sent him, time could have been saved. It was such a waste of resources, not to be confused with consumer protection, but that's the world we live in.

Q. If you had a chance to follow a different path, would you and what would it be?
A. Well, I would say that I would do the same thing again, but if I had to do something different my quick answer would be to get a PhD in economics and work as an economist for a bank or a consultant.

Q. What would you tell a college graduate with a degree in finance considering your chosen career?
A. A physician that I do not know well at all, but knows who I am, asks, "I have a son who is a finance major and he'd like to get into your field. Would you be willing to talk with him?" I said I would, so I do that sort of thing and have routinely over the years and I try to be very honest and straight forward with them.

I tell them that I like the business very, very much, but I also tell him that the truth is it's a hard business to get started in. It was hard when I got into it and am finding in a lot of ways that it's harder today. But I also tell them that as the industry is maturing. It's not like one person must be able to do it all. It helps to have a healthy combination of both the analytical, technical side of things as well as the marketing and sales ability. Today you have the larger firms which offer opportunity for those who are not necessarily gifted on both fronts.

Q. Do you feel the industry today is overly complicated and the products too few or too many?
A. I am enough of a believer in free markets that I am not going to say there are too few or too many products. I think there has been and will continue to be innovation and I think over time the companies that produce the better products

are likely to survive. It is certainly a challenge to stay on top of it all. We were a fairly early adaptor and have been using exchange-traded funds (ETFs) for our clients since 1999. We don't use them exclusively, but we like them. I would say that was a significant innovation and a good thing. We like the low expense ratios. We like the tax advantages and we do like to be able to trade during the day. That was not important to us initially. It became important to us during the credit crisis. Within these portfolios, most of what we do is fairly conventional – mutual funds and ETFs. We have used managed futures in a limited way. We've done very little with variable annuities. Mostly we have inherited them rather than initiate them. In the fall of 2008, on a very limited basis, we used ETFs that were leveraged and inverse ETFs. We were very fortunate in our use of them. We used very limited amounts, they are so high octane and dangerous that I can't imagine! We were fortunate.

Q. If you were looking at the current economy in relationship to somebody who is new in investing, or somebody who is an established investor, or lastly a retiree, how would you qualify this economy and how would you suggest they frame their expectations of it?

A. Well, for someone young, I would say it's quite possible that for a number of years the stock market might be a little sick. It may have problems, we may have some significant issues, we may have more deep down turns, but as long as you are investing regularly, you are going to be able to take advantage of those drops and buy shares of stock on sale and over time that will work out very well for you. So hang in there, think long term, and it should all work out well.

For the retirement age person with a shorter horizon, I would say that I am pretty sobered up by this economy and stock market, and even though I have typically been an optimist, I we need to be more cautious than normal. Yes, you do need a pretty healthy exposure to stocks, even in your retirement years, to make it work well, but today we want to be more cautious than normal. That's the kind of the language that I would use.

Q. What is your majority portfolio strategy for your clients?
A. Well, I was schooled in modern portfolio theory very, very thoroughly because I got my MBA from the University of Chicago, which was the pioneer in that arena. So I have used that philosophy over the years. I will admit that in the fall of 2008, as I started to understand what was going on, I did decide that we needed to make some cautionary moves. Even though I told people for years and years that you can't time the market, we did make significant defensive moves. But in general, I am still pretty comfortable with the primary tenants of the modern portfolio theory, but I still am open to other ideas and try to keep learning.

Q. Are you now following those investing decisions, are they predominantly made from intuition plus a good dose of the news; or have you adopted any other strategies in terms of trying to do market timing?
A. I would say that we do not have a scientific approach to it. I would say that I am very diligent in my reading. I try to stay very well informed and try to have an understanding of what is going on, but I am increasingly convinced that even if you have a pretty good understanding of what is going on, getting the timing right is extremely difficult. I think the timing of the crisis in the fall of 2008 in terms of the election was very interesting. I just say I am mindful of the fact that McCain and Obama were basically tied, and then we had this crisis and McCain simply wasn't prepared and he got clobbered.

Q. What does your average work week look like?
A. When my boys were growing up, I was probably only 60 to 70% focused on my business so I was able to take a lot of time to be with the family, to travel and do things together. When my younger son became a senior in high school, my wife and I started looking at where we were and what needed to happen for us to be where we wanted to be financially. We both

agreed that it was time for me to hit it hard. So I went from 60 to 70% to 150%, and stayed at 150% for four plus years. Now I am more like 100%. Most people have done it differently and worked harder in the early years. A typical workweek for me these days is 8:00 a.m. to 6:00 p.m. and most of Saturday if I am in town. I still do travel a fair amount. I still have a fair amount of vacation and flex time, but when I am in town I still hit it pretty hard. I am now 60 and eager to slow down some. I still enjoy my work, but I do have other interests. As much as I enjoy my work, I am excited about having more free time to do other things.

Q. As a business owner, what do you consider your most successful marketing strategy?

A. That has changed over time. We got quite a jump start in 2005 by doing seminars when Boeing was selling its commercial aircraft division in Wichita. There were many people who were leaving Boeing employment and had potential 401K roll-overs. We did seminars then to specifically target those people and it was certainly very successful. We have been fortunate enough to get a number of referrals over the years from some combination of existing clients, centers of influence, professionals, etc. That has really been the most important, but the seminars certainly help. In recent years we have done a fair amount of print advertising in a publication called East Wichita News. I have become at least somewhat branded in Wichita. I think that's been helpful too.

Q. How tough would you say your first three years were as a planner?

A. I would say very tough. My first association was with Mass Mutual the insurance company. I started out in insurance and securities and I was one of those guys who wanted to learn everything about everything before talking with anyone about anything. There were others that were willing to talk with everyone about anything without knowing very much about anything.

Probably three months into my training program with Mass Mutual they had a three-on-one meeting. The meeting was with the general agent, the assistant general agent, and the training director who said they had never seen anyone with such a slow start that had actually survived in this business. I told them, "I can't tell you exactly how I am going to do it and I don't doubt what you are saying, but I trust the Lord that this will work," and it did. But it was hard for me. I remember one of my early, early, conversations with a woman, who would later become my wife, back in 1981 when we were just getting acquainted. Mass Mutual actually cut off my draw. It was the kind of deal where when you get caught up on commissions you'd get whatever you hadn't gotten in a draw. I remember telling her that my pay had been cut off and I was running behind. It wasn't exactly an impressive thing to say to a woman I might want to marry, but she didn't say stop the car and let me out!

Q. If somebody said you could retire tomorrow, what does that actually mean to you?

A. To me it's an exciting thought, but premature. I am grateful for my work. What it would mean for me would be more time to be with family and friends, to be with people. Depending on where we were financially, it could mean more time to travel. We like to travel and we now have a little land just northeast of Wichita with a cabin we enjoy very much. I could see us spending more time out there, entertaining more, but my real passion is Jesus. I like the thought of more time reading the scriptures. I take very seriously the encouragement to love people, as does my wife, so we like the thought of just being friends to people. We value our relationships and take our relationships very seriously. Then the other thing is I would say I really do like to read. I like to learn.

There would be some pain for several reasons. Number one is I genuinely care for my clients. I enjoy my clients. I care about their financial future. I want the best for them and

I would truly miss them, so yes there would be some pain in walking away from those client relationships, but on the other hand I would be able to say that I never committed to being their financial advisor for my entire life.

Q. Do you have a succession strategy for your firm? We talked about your son earlier. He seems to stand out as a potential candidate.

A. We have worked on that, but nothing is nailed down. I have talked to another advisor on a contingency buy-sell agreement. That would only come into play in the event of a death or perhaps a disability. So assuming I stay healthy for a number of years, we do not yet have a plan, but I am starting to scratch my head and think about possibilities. I think the business will be a business that can and should be sold, and the purchaser would be wise to employ the team we have to retain clients better.

Q. If you had the opportunity to spend time with Bernie Madoff, what would you tell him?

A. Well, I have been forthright with you throughout this interview and I am going to do the same on this question. My answer may surprise you. If I had the opportunity to talk with him, I would say, "You know, the whole country knows that you made some terrible, terrible mistakes. I, Dick Coe, have also made some mistakes in my life. In fact, everyone has made big mistakes. You and I have both made mistakes," or I would use another word, "We both have sinned and the good news is that there is a man sent from God by the name of Jesus who died on the cross, paid a penalty for our sins. You may not believe it, but I want you to know that you are a human being, you are valued by God, and I care enough about you and your eternal destiny that I am willing to take this opportunity to tell you the good news about Jesus and if you want to hear more, I will tell you more. If you want me to be quiet, I will now be quiet."

Q. If there was one thing you could change in the industry what would it be?

A. I would say a prudent approach to regulation where the bad guys got punished and responsible people were able to operate their business in an economical way, helping more people.

Q. Is there anything else you would wish to add for the benefit of somebody who is considering our industry for their career?

A. I would say it is really a great business. I am only grateful for the privilege of having been in the business, for the opportunity it's provided to help people, the opportunity to learn, the opportunity to provide for myself and my family. I have enjoyed almost every day. Even the days that are sometimes frustrating for me in the overall scheme of things, have been pretty good days.

"The greatest challenge is regaining trust and pending legislation."
Michael Curtis, Curtis Financial Services

Michael Curtis has been involved with comprehensive financial planning for 35 years, starting out in 1975. Like many planners, he began in the life insurance industry with Northwestern Mutual Life Insurance Company (NML) at the age of 19. The strategy of helping clients provide for their families in the event of early death, while also making sure clients have money available when they need it most, led naturally into his work as an independent financial planner. After a long and successful career with NML, Michael left to start his own firm in October of 2006. He now manages approximately $60 million in assets. Michael operates his firm with his assistant, and in the near term hopes to expand with the addition of a junior advisor. Michael established himself and his firm with a bias toward money management.

Q. Was a career in financial planning an ambition when you were in college?
A. I attended college at night and had a great professor who took me aside and taught me how to invest. I still remember that first stock he recommended to me. It's interesting how life leads you down that path. My mistake was I should have gone directly into investment instead of insurance.

Q. After 30 plus years involved in this industry, you have obviously seen good and bad. What keeps you in the industry now?
A. I just love it. There is an old saying that if you want to be happy for a day, take the day off. If you want to be happy for a week, take a vacation. If you want to be happy for a year, retire, but if you want to be happy every day, have a job

where you enjoy getting up every day doing it. I just love this business. I love the people I work with, and my clientele is the best any advisor could ask for.

Q. When you meet with your clients today, what is the single greatest challenge that you face in meeting their needs and their expectations?

A. Today, it's trying to calm their fear after experiencing the free fall of the markets in 2008, especially if they had a relationship with another advisor they trusted. People lost a lot of money. Helping new potential clients regain their trust, and calming their fears of the markets is a great challenge these days. Not all advisors have that same mentality and ability to adapt to changing times. Down markets definitely outweigh up markets as to the effect it has on a client's portfolio. We are in a decade where we are slow in coming to that realization.

Q. Given your longevity in the business, what do you consider to be the greatest challenge facing the industry as a whole today?

A. The greatest challenge is regaining trust and pending legislation. Less than 1% of people in our business have created havoc for the rest of us, who are trying to do what's best in the interest of our clients and adhering to our fiduciary responsibilities. Most people have enough common sense to see that if it's too good to believe, than it's probably not true. Most potential investors have neither the patience or the time to read all the disclosures developed for their protection, so where's the benefit?

Q. What would also qualify as your greatest frustration with the industry?

A. I have seen a lot of advisors today concentrate more on marketing themselves than actually spending the time required for actively managing client's money. The client hired the advisor to manage their money and to oversee their financial stability and they should expect no less. When you hear these advisors speak at seminars, they say we should be concentrating more on marketing ourselves to grow the practice and then hire out the management of the money. I don't understand. I thought our main goal as advisors was to manage client's money efficiently and effectively. Because of their marketing abilities they might appear to be an expert in managing client's money, but most it seems are not actually taking an active role in money management. I feel many advisors are living in the markets of the 1980's and 1990's, where the skills of whether you were an effective manager were overshadowed by a market that was going up no matter what. It was hard to make mistakes during that period. The "modern portfolio theory" easily worked then, but today it doesn't in my opinion. Today you've got to really dig in and run ratios and do your homework. I grow my practice by managing money. If I can make 6% when the market is only making 2%, my assets under management increase as well as my income, and at the same time I take good care of my clients.

> *"I love the people I work with, and my clientele is the best any advisor could ask for."*

Q. If somebody stood in your office with a degree in finance and was looking for some direction in their career path, what would your advice be to them?

A. My advice for them would be to contact independent brokerage companies like Cambridge and ask, "Can you put me in contact with advisors who have successful practices and are in their 50s? Those who need to start looking for someone to bring in to transition their business down the road?" I know for a fact that there are many advisors out there who would love to be contacted and they offer a great opportunity to learn.

Q. When you look at the industry do you see it as being overly complicated in the product availability, with too few or too many?

A. The industry is very complicated, just like the medical field. I suggest that an advisor know his or her limitations and hire sub-advisors to fill those gaps. I see some advisors who try to go into endeavors for which they are just not qualified, and then get themselves into trouble. As far as products, I think there are sufficient products out there for whatever direction an individual wants to go and probably more products than there need to be.

Q. So talking about the economy and its machinations of interconnectivity globally, how significant is this to somebody that's just starting out, somebody that's established but twenty years from retirement, and somebody that's actually in retirement?

A. If they are close to retirement I think it's a very big detriment. It is essential their portfolios be managed by an active manager. In my opinion, in the next decade it's going to be tough to achieve returns at levels of the historical average of 10% per year. There's just no population growth in the U.S. or the world, and that is going to affect the amount of new money available to drive the markets and economy. The tax increases that our government is going to have to impose in the coming years will have a great impact on our economy and its ability to grow. It's going to be a very hard time, and it's going to be interesting trying to achieve returns for our clients.

We also have the problem of not having any interest rates to speak of to at least cover our exposure in the equity markets. We used to be able to get a 5% return in a money market account. We could take a 50% position in the market while getting a 5% return on the 50% held in a money market for example. If the 50% in the market lost 5% the 50% held in the money market offset the loss with its 5% gain. Nobody got hurt. Now we are just totally exposed when taking positions in the market by having few choices to offset that risk. It can be done, but you better know what you are doing. The old fixed income to equity ratios is not the answer these days.

Q. So if you were a 20-something year old, would you be loading up on equities right now or would you be advising people to take caution and hold a larger cash position, or bond position?

A. I would take caution because I don't see this market being great for some time. I'd sit back and wait for a good correction before getting fully invested into equity positions. I think it's a good time to be very defensive, because we've got so many issues out there that haven't been resolved yet. I feel the global debt crisis will only get worse. I see this next decade as a time not to get rich, but rather as a time just to make sure you don't lose money.

Q. So within your investment strategies, are you running modern portfolio theory? Are you actively managing? Is it sort of a hybrid of the two?

A. No. We've decided the modern portfolio theory needs to be put on the shelf for now. We are trying to focus on investments that have an opposite correlation to the market or have no correlation to the market in order to see if we can provide some protection to our equity positions. What has really helped us provide protection to date is that we were fortunate to buy a lot of discounted individual bonds for clients in 2008. Most of our clients over age 50 have positions in individual bonds of over 50%. We are very diversified in our holdings for client's, but the individual bonds have provided us the opportunity to be a bit more wet in the market. We can go through market volatility and still come out smelling like a rose.

> "Ninety-nine percent of advisors do have morals."

Q. What does your average work week look like?

A. My day starts off at home usually. By about 7 a.m. I'm checking premarket conditions as well as reading market related articles. I am usually in the office by 8:30 a.m. and work in the office till about 3:30 p.m. during the summer months. I am fortunate to have a 40 foot cruiser across the street from my office where I can continue my work day while doing any required research. The boat also comes in handy for client review meetings after 3:00 p.m. I feel it is very important that my clients are kept informed when it comes to their portfolios. I sometimes find myself sending them an e-mail at 2:00 a.m. and I will receive a call the next day stating, "Mike, what were you doing up that late? Get some sleep!" I monitor our e-mail address for the office 24/7, and clients are just amazed that I get back to them right away whether it is an evening or a weekend.

Q. What marketing strategy do you consider to be most successful? Do you also do specific marketing events?

A. I don't market. I probably should, but to date I just have not had the need. My clients do all the work for me. We have four to five call-ins a month and turn away several. Our clients like to share with friends and colleagues the experience they have working with us, as well as their investment returns. We make sure they fully understand what they are paying us to do and what they can expect to receive in return for our fees.

Q. What is your personal view of retirement for you and your family?

A. I am the oldest living male in my family. Most died of heart disease. So I will probably work until I die, but we have a buy-sell agreement in place and are presently training a potential junior advisor. Whoever I choose for the new advisor position will end up taking over the firm at my death, inheriting a great practice with an exceptional clientele. Having an in-house junior advisor eventually will allow me to know that things are under control if I am not around. Then I can enjoy my vacations a little bit more. So I will probably work from different locations until that day comes. I see a situation where I cut the cord for new business, the partner takes all the new clients, but I keep my core clients.

Q. If you have a chance to speak to Mr. Madoff, how would the conversation run?

A. I would ask him why he felt the need to rob people of their livelihoods. He had enough presence in the business that he didn't have to do what he did in order to make a good living. Why did you have to ruin people's lives, ruin the reputation of our industry, and take your greed to levels that caused the demise of many, many people? The other thing is that you must not believe in another world or a superior spirit because if you did, you would not have chosen the road that awaits you now.

Q. If there was one thing in the industry that you could change, what would it be?

A. It would be receiving more trust from government and recognition that clients are smarter than they think they are. Ninety-nine percent of advisors do have morals, do have a conscience and are trying to do what's best for their clients and are in compliance.

Q. Would there be any last comment or advice for people considering this as a career?

A. Always put your client's interests first and your practice will fall into place and grow. Be sincere, provide your client's with the service they deserve and have every right to expect from you, and educate them so they truly understand. A lot of clients come in from other firms and cannot believe how much information we provide them with.

"Retirement is not the cessation of work, but the cessation of toil. Work is creative—and ceasing to be creative is death. Work is fulfilling; toil is drudgery. Work is choice; toil is no choice. So retirement is having greater choices and the resources to creatively pursue them. Retirement is working to fulfillment, not to the point of drudgery. Retirement is working to the finish, not finishing your work."

-Ben Coombs

"Many advisors are good at giving financial advice, but they aren't typically good at running a business."

Vinton Fountain, Fountain Financial Associates

Vinton Fountain has been in the financial services business for 26 years and has had his own investment and financial planning company for the past 12 years. Vinton is a former banker, and spent 16 years in banking before the start up of his own firm. His firm has eight employees and currently has $200 million in assets under management. Vinton's employees are specialists in income planning, retirement income planning, and estate/tax work.

Q. Was a career in the financial services industry a childhood ambition for you?
A. No. I had no idea. I was a political science major in college, which was supposed to be pre-law. My family owned a business in my home town, so I thought I would go home to work for my father. Essentially it was, "Okay Dad, I am ready to come home to work," but he said, "Well, I don't have a job for you." I noticed that a bank was interviewing on campus and so I decided to give it a shot. The employer happened to be one of the best training organizations in the financial services world at the time, which I learned by accident, and they made an offer. I realized it was a great place to start in financial services, and that's how I got into banking. I started in retail, but also did commercial banking. I actually started my first week as a teller at a branch bank, which is the way it was done back in those days. It was the start at the bottom and earn your way up model. You've got to balance a teller window before you can be CEO.

Q. So what was it that motivated you to start your own firm, specifically as a financial planner? What was the epiphany moment?

A. I was recruiting traditional stockbrokers to work inside the bank. The great opportunity for the banking industry at the time was, "We need to build investment competency. We know how to lend money, now we need to diversify the revenue base and become a full-service firm where we can make loans, manage assets, sell insurance, etc." As I recruited financial advisors from large institutions such as Smith Barney, Merrill-Lynch, and UBS, I became intrigued and fascinated with the industry. As I gained insight into how the industry worked, I realized that there was an opportunity for independent advice and the market was screaming for an alternative to the traditional stockbroker model.

> "How is the regulatory environment going to evolve to support our system, our free enterprise system?"

Q. So what do you see as the greatest challenge in meeting your client's needs?

A. The greatest challenge at the moment is their lack of confidence in the world today. I believe we, as a nation, have a severe self-esteem problem. One of the things I like about this industry is that it is so dynamic. The challenges are different every day, every month, every year and every decade.

Today, there is a breakdown of confidence in the system and the industry of financial services. It's the lack of economic confidence, the fear of our political system, the lack of investment confidence, Wall Street, the whole thing. People are scared, they're traumatized. They know they need help more than ever, which is a good thing for those of us in the business. They are starting to appreciate the value of independence, which is positive for those of us in the business, but still, at the end of the day, they've got to get help navigating the terrain that they are in now, particularly the people who are over 50.

Q. So when you are faced with a younger client, in the early stages of a career, what's the most important piece of advice you would give them?
A. Saving. That is universally my investment tip for everybody that asks. Individuals control their success more than they think. By focusing on the things that you do control, such as lifestyle and good habits like saving money, you can influence your success more than anything else. So when I am speaking to someone who's in that place in life, I am going to encourage them to develop good habits which would include a methodical savings pattern with assistance from someone who can help them monitor how you are doing.

Q. What do you see as the greatest challenge facing the industry?
A. Today, it's regulatory. How is the regulatory environment going to evolve to support our system, our free enterprise system? Is it going to be effective or not? None of us really know the answer to that question, but that is my primary concern. I fear that the problems that occurred in our industry will result in regulatory changes that will reshape the way financial advice is delivered. It might also make it more expensive and harder for an independent firm to deliver that advice. So that's one thing that keeps me up at night. The largest risk a successful independent advisor faces is the regulatory risk within our industry. It's the things out of our control that concern me the most.

Q. Do you see the industry as being clearly delineated and well understood by the clients?
A. The quick answer would be not really because they have a hard time understanding what's different about working at

> *"I believe we, as a nation, have a severe self-esteem problem."*

a big Wall Street firm versus you. Before you teach them, they don't tend to get it right away, but I think as you have seen the transformation take place. Let's face it, Merrill-Lynch was one of the finest brands in the world and their model collapsed for whatever reason. So that's the kind of change that people are observing and beginning to understand. Why did that model not work? The more people see that happen, the more they will understand the value of independence. I watch the ads on T.V. for the big firms, and I keep saying, "The big guys are going to teach clients that independence is good." Schwab and others – with their sound bites and their massive budgets are slowly teaching people the value of independence. I think, "This is beautiful because that's going to help them and it's going to help our independent model." Back in the old days it was, "Well, I've got to go with whoever has the biggest, shiniest brand." That has changed.

Q. What advice would you give a college graduate with a degree in finance?

A. Look within. Don't get started in the industry just yet. Get focused on YOU first. Understand where your genius lies. Do you like technical quantitative work? Or do you like something different? Marketing? Sales? Talking to a lot of people? Think strategically. I tell them to go ahead and spend a lot of time understanding who you are, how you are wired, where your gift is, and what do you not enjoy doing? Once you get those answers, you can begin figuring out how to plot a path in this industry. That's my typical first conversation with someone who is really raw and just at the beginning stages of learning about the industry.

Then, after they have some self-awareness around their skill sets and their own wiring, we can go the next step. Usually that tends to pivot them either into the technical research of our industry, or the people interactive human side of the business.

Q. Do you feel the industry today is overly complicated and just the sheer collection of products and strategies is too few or too many?
A. I do think that people have difficulty navigating the complexity of the industry and so it does become a hurdle for advisors and the public. However, the tools and resources that are available to advisors are tremendous. I don't know that you can go too far in terms of having different tools to help you implement the kinds of things you need to do to have financial success. Do I use everything? Absolutely not. For example, I haven't used hedge funds, and I'm happy about that. Part of my job is to navigate that complexity, weed out the stuff that's not appropriate, or what I am not comfortable with, and just use the things that I am comfortable with. Yes, there's a lot of complexity, but I like it in a way because it gives me a lot of choices and enables me to make sure that I have a full tool box to help clients.

> *"...if it seems too good to be true, it probably is, and I have used that example as a talking point with clients who become over-ambitious about performance returns."*

Q. This next question is sort of a three-way and it relates specifically to our current economy. How significant do you feel either the opportunity or the severity relates to firstly a new investor, then an established investor, and lastly a retiree?
A. Each of these three groups have different objectives. The new investor tends to be an accumulator, someone who is getting started, has income, debt, and needs to build net worth. So for them, I think the economy is kind of a treasure chest of opportunities, global investing, and new technologies. That's the new.

For the established investor, it is a little harder because people are trained to buy the blue chips with the good dividends but have learned that doesn't always work. So we are in a transition of globalization of the economies of the world.

Retirees are security and income oriented, whether they know it or not. They have the pressures of inflation, taxes and longevity risk. These folks are in protection mode as a rule of thumb. They need to protect, preserve and create income. In their case the new economy is obviously scary, and even scarier because of principal volatility. They need more support than most demographic groups because the challenges are greater and coaching is more important.

Q. In your portfolios, do you use third-party money managers or do you work on your own portfolio management?
A. I prefer the former, which is using outside managers, either funds or separate accounts. My model is to engage with the needs of clients and allow others to understand India, China, and so on and so forth. Advisors should be wary of the trap of being all things to all people. I don't know anyone who can do it all in-house effectively.

Q. Within their portfolios, do you just leave that completely to the money managers? Do you steer it in any way?
A. Yes, I provide guidance on the strategic decisions such as financial planning, taxes and inflation. I build a roadmap for the client and then monitor their progress. The research and security selection is done by outside managers.

Q. So, do you consider the greater challenge managing your clients or managing your company?
A. At the moment, clients. My banking experience helped me understand how to run a business, which was an advantage over a lot of financial advisors. Many advisors are good at giving financial advice, but they aren't typically good at running a business. So that was a real lucky break for me. Right now the business is not hard to run. The advice component,

the coaching, is the most difficult because of all of the external conditions that we discussed earlier. Clients need coaching now more than ever.

Q. So, with that said, what is your personal average work week look like?

A. Well, it's gotten much better. I am probably working 30 hours in the office, and 10 per week at my home office, a separate building from my home and functional as a traditional office. Of course, every business owner knows that it is 24 hours a day, 7 days a week. You never turn it off.

Q. What would you consider to be your most successful marketing strategy?

A. Publishing articles, newsletters, interviews, media, those kinds of things, but I am referring to the macro publishing of articles for newspapers, etc. I am writing a monthly article for a women's magazine and I am going to do six months of that. I am also attempting to be a resource for media outlets in terms of content. I recently got a call from the local newspaper. They were working on a story and wanted me to help with some Q&A. They need experts. I enjoy writing, but did not learn this until I got into this business. I enjoy it and it's effective from a client development stand point.

Q. How tough were your first three years when you broke away from the bank?

A. I would say extremely difficult. I was trying to come up with an analogy and the best one is from the movie Gladiator. Russell Crowe fights tigers, barbarians, and the like in the Roman Colosseum. That's pretty much what it's like. It's very difficult and scary, but at the same time very motivating, and that's where the passion comes in. If you don't have the passion, if you don't have that conviction of who you are, what you do, how you do it, and why it matters, you will never make it through those first three years. On the other hand, if you do have it, then once you get through those first three years you will see enough success that you will build confidence. So eventually the fear gets replaced with confidence and then it just kind of snowballs.

Q. So what is your personal view of retirement?
A. You know I enjoy this work. It is very rewarding to help people in this way, so my idea would be to always be involved and have a succession plan that allows others to step in and sort of run things. I can be more of a facilitator and someone who is engaged when needed, but completely at my choosing, and sort of work down that path. I am only 51 so I probably will continue to go pretty strong for five to ten more years minimum, and then start to get out of the way and let some of the young folks come in and do it.

Q. What is your expectation for the firm at that point? Do you have a succession strategy or do you have partners?
A. I would like to participate in the transition with the people who are in the firm, helping them build and continue growing the firm, thus allowing me to share in the equity that I built. It would be great to also allow them an opportunity to own the equity which offers them the same kind of benefits that I have enjoyed. I guess it's a transition strategy that involves the people that are currently building the firm, allowing the ownership to transfer in an orderly fashion, over a period of time.

Q. If you had the chance to sit with Bernie Madoff, what would you tell him?
A. Well, I would not have any kind words. He has certainly done extensive damage to a lot of people and to our industry. I don't know how he can live with that, but at the same time I would try to maintain some level of forgiveness. He has certainly been a disgrace and what he did is despicable. The learning lesson is if it seems too good to be true, it probably is, and I have used that example as a talking point with clients who become over-ambitious about performance returns.

Q. So if there was one thing you could change in our industry, what would it be?

A. I guess it would be the misguided information that creates a lack of trust. It's kind of a catch-22. A lot of us in our business pick on the media because there is so much ratings-driven sensationalism. Poor quality information can damage an individual's success and security. So that's probably the answer to the question, but on the back side of that, our business thrives as a result of people needing to get good coaching and counseling. The media creates demand for advisors.

Q. Do you have any last comments on the industry?

A. What an opportunity for those of us who can be effective in helping clients with one of the most important aspects of their lives: their families, their future, their money, their security, reducing anxiety and stress, and allowing them to reach their full potential. I mean, it's really pretty phenomenal. For those who do it right, remain ethical and succeed in their promise to help others, I just can't think of a better profession.

"The business of life is life, not business."

-Floyd Green

"It takes a long time to build to a point of professional success and economic success in this industry. So if you are looking for it to grow very quickly, this may not be the industry for you."
Steve Girard, Northstar Financial Companies, Inc.

Steven is the president of Northstar Financial Companies, Inc., and the principal investment advisor representative of the firm. With over 18 years of financial planning experience, he believes that financial planning is the key to achieving a life lived well. He founded Northstar Financial Companies, Inc. in Boston, MA as an independent registered representative in 1994. Today, Northstar manages $150M and is both an RIA and registered representative of its broker dealer.

Q. Was a career as a financial planner a childhood ambition?
A. As a childhood ambition, no. My ambitions to become a financial planner didn't start until I was out of college. I went to college to study English with the intention of getting into the advertising industry. I had actually wanted to work in the art department of an advertising agency and I interned at a couple places in Boston, but it never amounted to anything. I had a ton of job interviews for the advertising industry and didn't get hired by anybody. I wound up with a public relations job for a home health visiting nurse agency. One of the people that worked there had a friend who worked for MetLife, I wasn't making much money and he approached me with an opportunity to work for them.

Q. So it really wasn't an ambition?
A. No – I had always been interested in the stock market and my father and I used to talk about it a bunch, but it had never been something I had thought was going to be a career.

Q. So what is your greatest motivation for remaining a financial planner?
A. At this point it would be to progress the elements of what I think a financial planning firm in this day and age should be.

Q. Which is what?
A. I always say something of size and substance, so something that has both the ability to provide a high quality service to any and all clients no matter what their level of asset, wealth or knowledge. As well as one that has a voice in the industry to be able to promote our opinions on things to the financial planning industry as a whole, so both for clients and for adding direction to the industry.

Q. What is the greatest challenge in meeting client needs?
A. Expectations. Often I think it's a no-win industry, where in good times it tends to be the client's recommendations or ideas or stock picks that work best, and then in the down years it's always our recommendations or ideas that do the worst. So I would go back to the market creating an emotional backdrop affecting the client, this is something that becomes hard to control. So keeping our clients on an even keel through both good times and bad times, good times we have to keep them calm and not perpetually euphoric, and bad times make them understand it will turn around.

Q. When addressing a new investor, what is the single most important piece of advice you would offer?
A. Start somewhere and the earlier you start the better. Just get into the habit of managing your finances and your long-term goals at a very early age, just start. Start somewhere and get into the habit and then build from there. If they are in a position or in a firm that has a 401(k), I think it's the easiest place for them to begin because it can be habit-forming, just because they are saving it out of their paycheck and it makes it easier. From a planning basis, I would much prefer they were maxing out a ROTH contribution. I think there's far

more inherent value to them in the long run on that, but just getting them to be motivated and interested in their finances and growing their money and accumulating – I think a 401(k) is a great place to start.

Q. So what's the greatest challenge facing the industry?
A. Image; a perceived level of professionalism, changing the image from being considered a bunch of people who didn't have anything else going on in their life so they became insurance agents who then became financial planners and elevating that to the level of accountant or attorney. In part, the industry creates its own problems. As an example, here we are now having discussions about certain share classes being bad for clients and the level of fee-disclosures. These are all things the industry created itself. I think the industry at times needs to standardize a lot of how it gets compensated and then promote that. The industry at times is its biggest impediment.

> *"Just get into the habit of managing your finances and your long-term goals at a very early age, just start."*

Q. What frustrates you most about the industry?
A. The attitude of many planners being, "Me first, then the client." I am not saying that's everybody, but I think it's prevalent. I think there are a greater percentage of planners that are more about what they are making in a given year, than what they are doing for clients. If they would embrace it in the other way, they ultimately would make the same amount of money or more and everybody would win.

Q. Looking back, if you had a chance to follow a different path, would you and what would you do?
A. Are some days frustrating and do periods of time like 2008 and 2009 make you shake your head, yes absolutely. In overall terms do I wish I had created a different career path for myself ? No. This is an extremely rewarding career, when

somebody recognizes what you have done for them and when you see the fruits of your labors it's a wonderful feeling. The income potential is very real for those who are able to hang in through the early years, remain ethical and not lose sight of what it is they do – it's a great career.

Q. What would you tell a college graduate with a degree in finance considering this as a career?

A. That's a really good question. I would say, "If you are going to enter a career of financial planning, expect it to be a building process; your own personal success will not happen right away. It takes a long time to build to a point of professional success and economic success in this industry. So if you are looking for it to grow very quickly, this may not be the industry for you. I think you have to really step back and judge what kind of personality you are. Do you want to interact with people on a daily basis, have discussions with them about their personal life, about their finances? Do you want to deal with the emotionality of clients, both good and bad? If that's the kind of work or interaction you don't want to have on a daily basis, then you may be better off in a more analytical kind of role."

Q. Do you feel the industry is overly complicated and the products too many?

A. Yes. Again, I go back to the industry creating its own issues and it creates its own complexities by being too creative at times. If you go back to the basics, even though the last number of years have been difficult, vanilla still works. I think that while there are some worthwhile and creative products coming out, I think at times we could have far less if they were much more vanilla in their approach.

Q. What is the majority portfolio strategy for your clients?

A. I am still a believer in core, long-term buy and hold, core modern portfolio theory, but I think that it needs to be coupled with more active and proactive satellite holdings. I think that even your long-term hold stuff needs to be proactively managed and not just put it in place and forget about it. You have to manage the quality of the investments that you own. I believe that a diverse portfolio, in the long run, still proves itself out to be the way to go and that would include stocks, bonds, real estate, precious metals, and other alternatives from there. I don't think it takes 100 holdings; I think you can still have a really solid portfolio with 10, 12, 15 holdings and you would be fine.

Q. What does your average work week look like?
A. You don't really have a beginning and end of a work day, especially if you are an independent financial planner. It sort of carries itself throughout the day, whether it be a client calling you at odd hours or an email coming in that you are going to answer. So I would say my work day is kind of fluid and never ending. It's a mix of planning, asset-management, client service, client touches; it's a pretty diverse mix every day.

Q. So how many hours a week do you think you work?
A. That's a good question...I don't know...60-80?

Q. What would you consider your most successful marketing strategy?
A. Me! I have never been one that has done marketing programs and carried them on and on and on, we have done seminars but not perpetually. I would say that our best marketing strategy has been acquiring other practices and making them better. When we buy a book of business, we endeavor to make the book better. We increase the level of service and business we do within them.

Q. How tough were the first three years as a planner?
A. Horrible! I mean, I began my career at MetLife and I can remember sort of my watershed moment of deciding whether I was going to continue on or not. I was on a financing plan with MetLife and I think it at my third or fourth quarter that

I was with them, I had a bunch of business actually come off the books. My manager called me and said, "Hey, I just want to let you know that for the next 13 weeks, your take-home pay is going to be $75 a week." So I had a conversation with my father that night and my father said, "Are you sure you really want to do this?" And I said, "Yeah, I really do." That was the toughest period of time I think. It was always tough slog, especially in the early part as you were trying to build the clientele, you had no reputation, you had no one that really knew you and you were just out there hitting everything you could and talking to everyone you could. It was not easy.

> *"If everybody is paid the same percentage of anything they do, on any piece of business they do, you would completely eliminate any selling of things that are not right for a client."*

Q. What is your view of retirement – your own personal view of retirement?

A. I would say that I am one of these guys where retirement for me is not something where I am continuing on in this industry. When I am done and retiring, I will be done and moving on to do other things that I want to do in my life. If I have learned anything from the acquisitions we have done, it is that the seller who stays on after the initial period of transition becomes frustrated, the buyer becomes frustrated and in general, it's a bad situation. I would not wish to be part of the buyer's organization for longer than necessary.

Q. If you had the opportunity to talk to Bernie Madoff, what would you say?

A. I would probably say, "Thanks a lot for making my life harder." I would say, "You greedy b'stard." I wouldn't have much to say to him because he disgusts me.

Q. Do you agree there should be a standardized, minimum qualification to call yourself a planner?

A. Yes. When I talked about professionalism earlier, I think that there needs to be more than just going out and passing my series 7. Do I think it needs to be to the level where everybody has to pass their CFP? Maybe, because if you look at the accounting industry – and I could be wrong on this – but I am fairly certain you need to pass your CPA exam in order to be called an accountant. Now that's going to change the industry model. You're not going to have insurance companies bringing in a hundred guys off the street and putting them out to work collecting what they can and then losing 99% of them. You would bring everyone in this business to a level equal to being a CPA or an attorney, and that would be viewed much more favorably.

Q. Lastly, if there would be one thing you could change about the industry, what would it be?

A. This is being broad – if I were to change one thing, I would have everybody be compensated the same. If everybody is paid the same percentage of anything they do, on any piece of business they do, you would completely eliminate any selling of things that are not right for a client. You would completely avoid this idea of a person gouging their client. You would all be compensated the same and now it would come down to your skill level as to what you would do for clients, both on a planning and service basis. As a planner and an asset-gatherer, if you are getting paid a flat fee, 1% of the assets and there are no commissions, no 12-B-1's, no renewals, it was purely a flat fee that you were being paid, now it comes down to those of us that do really great work gathering assets because we do the things that clients are looking for. You would avoid things like overselling of annuity products to clients because the rep is just looking to make a big hit.

"The life insurance industry hijacked financial planning in the 1970s, and the tax shelter industry hijacked it in the 1980s. In the 1990s, it was hijacked by the asset management industry. I wonder who's next?"

-James Helba

"Unfortunately, investors at times just want to believe in 'too good to be true' things."
John Grillo, Grillo and Associates

John has been involved in the financial planning industry for 15 years. A mechanical aerospace engineer, John was working in a successful company in a senior role when he was struck by a desire to change careers while studying for an MBA. Today John operates a successful business with 3 staff members. Today they are managing in excess of $150M.

Q. So what field of engineering were you in?
A. I was in design engineering for fluid flow – first hydraulic flow and eventually the flow of blood through blood cell counters. That was the industry I was in; my employer was Coulter Corporations, now Coulter Beckman.

I loved the engineering field and was fortunate enough to be granted two United States patents for my design work. About two years out of engineering school I went back nights for an MBA with a concentration in finance. In the program at the University of Connecticut, I met a woman, Marlane Richter who was a CFP. I was just really impressed with her practice so when I finished my MBA I started the CFP courses through the College of Financial Planning. While completing my CFP nights I accepted the position with Coulter Corporation in Florida. The most ironic thing is that my dad was an advisor for New York Life for 50 years and never pushed any of his three boys in that direction. He let his three boys follow our passion – and I had now found mine in the financial planning field. It was still very difficult to quit a successful career and enter a new field. Fate came into play when in 1994 hurricane Andrew came through South Florida. We were living on the Intracoastal Waterway, so we had to evacuate. We loaded up our newborn little girl and we went up to the New York Life's national conference in Orlando. I attended many of the presentations, and that was the tipping point for me. I went back a month after that and gave my notice and started my practice. My wife Robyn, my daughters Emma and I, moved up to Connecticut to learn the ropes from my father.

Q. So there was no legacy from your father whatsoever?
A. As far as legacy, my father was an incredible mentor but did not initially provide me with any clients. His view was one of "You can feed a man a fish for a day, but are better off teaching a man how to fish for a lifetime." Although it was quite painful financially, he made the perfect decision. Learning how to prospect in this business is the number one key to success. One winter in Connecticut, convinced Robyn and I, that we had to return to warmer climates. We made our last move to Carrollton, Ga in 1996. Carrolton was my wife's hometown. I joined rotary and started coaching soccer, and started my practice. I thought with my MBA and CFP that clients would be knocking my door down – I was in for a rude awakening. This business takes prospecting and building trusting relationships.

> "The greatest challenge we see are really the media and the amount of misinformation out there – something said by Cramer on CNBC becomes immediate fact."

Q. What motivates you the most about being a planner?
A. New York Life is a tremendous company. I obviously wanted to be a financial planner having gone through the CFP program, but the tipping point was to listen to real life stories of a widow who was helped by her financial advisor. He had done a complete plan for the family and had encouraged adequate life insurance. When the husband prematurely passed away, the surviving spouse was able to put her children through school and pay off her mortgage and maintain

a comfortable lifestyle. The process of organizing and guiding clients through their financial plan was very appealing. What a wonderful thing to earn a living and be able to help people in that fashion. Shortly after I started in the business, I worked with a man who was a diplomat for the United Nations. Unfortunately he did not have a great relationship with his wife, and I could not get them to buy life insurance. After a great deal of persuasion I encouraged each of them to purchase term insurance to protect their family. They ended up getting a divorce and shortly after the divorce he moved to South America. She received custody of the children, but within months she passed away from cancer. That was the first life death benefit I had to deliver. We had set up a trust for her two girls and we have been using the proceeds to put the girls through college. There's just nothing better than helping a family save for their children's education, their own retirement, or helping to protect surviving family members through the use of insurance.

Q. So what do you see as the greatest challenge with meeting client needs or expectations?
A. The greatest challenge we see are really the media and the amount of misinformation out there – something said by Cramer on CNBC becomes immediate fact. Investors, at times, tend to take as fact what they hear on CNBC or FOX news. Investors also tend to chase historic returns, as exemplified by the latest DALBAR study. The last couple of years they were chasing real estate and now they are chasing gold. It is my job to filter out all the noise and misinformation and keep them focused on their goals. We get so many questions on gold today and we try, in a logical manner, to make them understand why gold is purely a speculative investment. Somebody has to want to have it; there's no real use except for jewelry and maybe some electronics. So I think that's our greatest challenge. It's really just dealing with misinformation.

Q. Have you found the pervasive nature of media in the last three years affecting clients more?

A. I started my career in 1995 when online access was just warming up. The Internet and access to information is now blazing. This makes it difficult for an advisor. Clients can have access to information quickly through news or Internet. At times this information is incomplete or taken out of context. This can lead to poor or emotional decisions. Warren Buffett once said that investing is about fear and greed. I think the media just magnifies this for the investing public.

Q. What do you think is the greatest challenge facing the industry?

A. I talked about media, but another issue is compliance. Unfortunately a few bad people like Bernie Madoff made good ethical advisors lives more difficult. Every time we turn around we have multiple i's to dot and t's to cross. One of the things in the engineering industry that kind of pushed me away was spending 80% of my time on paperwork. I don't know what Obama has in store for us, but more and more regulation makes, for those ethical planners, our job tougher and tougher. It will ultimately just increase the cost for clients. The level of uncertainty is something we are going to have to live with; we are just going to have to embrace it.

> "I know we are going to be short on advisors in the future, but making sure someone has to go through accreditation, whether it's a CFP, or some sort of training, CHFC, to make sure that their credentials would be important."

Q. Did you ever have any boyhood dreams to do anything different?

A. I was always an engineer. I was always ripping things apart, putting things back together – trying to figure things out and solve puzzles. I also love teaching and coaching. Financial planning allows me to satisfy both desires. I can gather and solve a client's plan and then teach and coach them on the implementation.

Q. Do you feel the industry has become overly complicated?
A. Life has become over complicated. We all have just too many choices. I believe this provides advisors with job security. It is our job to simplify the product offerings and decipher them for our clients. I will give an example of equity-indexed annuities. I love to analyze them because we are having clients who hear on the radio, "Would you like to get a guaranteed 8% average return with no downside?" I enjoy tearing them apart to see how they really work and explain to clients what they are ultimately getting. Unfortunately, investors at times just want to believe in 'too good to be true' things.

Q. Do you make use of all the available products, particularly ETFs?
A. In some form or fashion. Most of our models are utilizing mutual funds; we have a couple models that utilize an ETF as a hub and the spokes are using the active managed funds. We use symmetry, which are basically indexed funds. It depends on the client. If the client just does not believe in active management, we will use an ETF model to create that portfolio allocation. I don't have to necessarily convince them because no one is going to know for ten years whether active or passive was the right way to go. If I can get a client extremely well diversified, he does not have to use the active managed portfolios that I have put together.

Q. So when you look at the economy as it is currently, and cast it back three years, how significant do you feel it is to the new investor, the established investor, and the retiree?
A. Whether it's a new investor, established, or a retiree, I think the significance is in their emotion, for our clients at least. In 2007, only because we were concerned about the real estate market and sub-prime, we rebalanced our clients to make them more conservative. In hindsight I would have gotten

them much more conservative. But I think the significance of the economy has just put enormous fear into rational people. Investors are not thinking in terms of ups and downs, they are thinking about losing everything. It is my job as an advisor to put fears like this into perspective. I tried to explain to clients: as you drive from here to Atlanta and you pass Hewlett Packard, you pass Home Depot, and you pass Coca Cola – these are the positions that make up your portfolio. What would your portfolio look like if all those companies were out of business? But if these companies are all out of business and these people are no longer employed, not paying taxes to the government, then the government doesn't have the ability to back the FDIC. So the thought of taking everything I have out of this well-diversified portfolio and sticking it in an FDIC insured account makes less sense. After the fact, our clients are thanking us for helping them stay the course. My glass is always half full and I think we are going to have a tremendous 10 or 15 years.

Q. Are you steering clients who run a DCA program to put more in now than perhaps they would have done?

A. If a client has a specific asset allocation and there's going to be another down-turn and events like another terrorist event, people are just not going to have the stomach to handle another 30% downturn. So if a client's allocation can allow them to meet their goals, I am not going to get greedy.

Q. Do you see the emotional baggage of the recent market affecting younger investors?

A. We only have about 1,500 participants in 401K plans, and a handful – maybe 10% of those participants – stopped participating even though we were explaining the ideas of buying low and selling high. Then I had some client's that stopped adding to their kid's 529 plans and have since come back and said, "Well, you said that was a mistake and I guess that was a mistake." Emotion drives everything. Buffet said, "Be fearful when others are greedy and greedy when others are fearful." It's not logical, but many investors just do the wrong thing.

Q. Did your portfolio structures and strategies change through that period of time, or did you try to maintain that diversification and allocation model?
A. We pretty much shifted. Anyone that was close to retirement or on the verge of retirement in 2007, we did a shift to a more conservative asset allocation. I thought that would give us some protection and if things did not correct then we would still have some opportunity for upside. After the market downturn, we started pulling just out of the fixed income side of our retired clients' portfolios to give their stocks a chance to grow. We have now shifted back to taking distributions across the entire portfolio allocation.

Q. So what is the safest piece of advice you can give somebody in the early stages of their career as a planner?
A. One, to be prepared financially. If you are just getting out of college, find a great mentor. We have a young advisor in a support role in our firm and you can see that he's going to make it. He's learning how to analyze data, design plans, and speak correctly to clients. As soon as he is ready, he will become an advisor. He and his wife are socking away some savings now; he knows he is not going to have the salary that he has today once he goes into that industry.

Q. What does your average work week look like?
A. What is great is I don't think I have ever missed a child's sporting event, or a musical event or any of their activities. Our work is very flexible if you have proper staff. Now a typical work week in the office is maybe 30 to 35 hours in the office, but my work never stops. With the technology we have, we can work anytime, anywhere. So it's really hard. If someone thinks they are going to get into this industry and work 20 or 25 hours a week and that's it, it's just not going to happen. You can never stop working, especially since you can

always look at the market, you can do research, you can do just about anything, anywhere, at any time.

Q. Do you do marketing?
A. No. When we first moved to Carrolton, I started coaching the kids. There wasn't money from the community to buy their T-shirts, so we purchased the team shirts and had Grillo and Associates T-shirts running all over the county. You can still see them, there's just thousands and thousands of T-shirts and that's the only marketing we have ever done. We do have a website, but our main marketing system is asking for referrals. I always ask for referrals at the end of every client meeting.

Q. How difficult was the first three years having sold all your assets?
A. The first year I was in the business, nine or ten months into it, we had gone through maybe $50,000 of savings. I had a nice 401K, but I told my wife that basically I would go back to engineering before we encroached upon our 401K. One day in November of 1995 I was having a weak moment and received a call with an offer to come back to Coulter Corporation. Considering the beautiful beaches of Fort Lauderdale and the cold grey weather of New England, I decided to seriously consider the offer. It was very difficult and we were almost out of savings. My father encouraged me to continue prospecting and to have faith. He gave us a small loan to make it through the rest of the year and from that point things just fell into place. That was the transition point. The next year my confidence increased and my fear diminished – and that comes across to clients too. Now my fear is succession. If something happens to me, if I passed away, who takes over this practice?

Q. What is your personal view of retirement?
A. I just can't imagine retiring – right now I do everything I want to do. I have two children and one of them may have the

aptitude and the interest to come into the business, but as my dad did with his three boys, I am going to let them follow their own dreams. My ideal view is that I would still be in the business and we would have our staff and children take over and handle more clients as I step back a little bit.

Q. What are your opinions on Mr. Madoff?
A. It's funny because I thought when he did that, how dare him take that trust and destroy it. When I was working as a design engineer, people may have questioned my calculations, the theory, whatever, but my integrity was never questioned. Then to come into this business and to love it and to be caring for clients and to have jerks like Madoff create suspicion. I never had a client question me about my integrity until Madoff pulled his stunt. That's the hardest thing to handle in this industry, when someone questions your integrity. Even when you are trying to put in place a term life policy and someone might say, "Are you doing this because of the commission?" Normally my response is, "Whether you buy this policy or not, my lifestyle doesn't change at all, but your family will sure be grateful having put this in place." So Madoff just created more skepticism and worry on the part of clients that this sort of thing could happen.

> *"We do have a website, but our main marketing system is asking for referrals. I always ask for referrals at the end of every client meeting."*

Q. If there is one thing you could change in this business, what would it be?
A. I guess this is selfish since I am a CFP, but the barriers to entry – you get the village idiot that is aggressive and impersonal and selling products like viatical agreements and equity indexed annuities and things like that. I know we are going to be short on advisors in the future, but making sure someone

has to go through accreditation, whether it's a CFP, or some sort of training, CHFC, to make sure that their credentials would be important.

Q. Anything else you would add?
A. Our whole job is not to build great wealth for clients; it is to make sure they have the means to fulfill their dreams. Make sure clients put their moneys to good use. They cannot take it with them.

"There are still plenty of guys in the field who don't really know anything, but represent themselves as planners."
Sheldon Harber, Asset Strategies, Inc.

Sheldon has been in the financial planning industry for 31 years. He has two guys locally that each have their own office, and a couple of staff members. In terms of assets being managed he has about $100M. Sheldon considers himself to be a generalist and tries to do a lot of work with allied professionals.

Q. Was a career as a financial planner a childhood ambition?
A. My father got into the insurance business in 1958 and financial planning. I was able to watch him growing up, and it always interested me. Sometimes my dad would take me on a Saturday morning to work with him. I can even remember him going to collect premiums for a couple of clients. I probably even went with him on a death claim. That is sort of an interesting part of the business, really how the whole thing got rolling because that was back in '68 and he took the check, the death claim check, to the widow and handed it to her and she said, "Well what do I do with this?" And the light bulbs went off. I went to college thinking I was going to be a CPA until I took the first test and then I said, "Hmm...I think I will be a financial planner."

Q. So what is your greatest motivation for being a financial planner at this point in your career?
A. At this point I am trying to get to the next step where I can get enough money that I can give away to my favorite causes.

Q. What do you see as being your greatest challenge in meeting your clients' needs?

A. I think it is managing expectations. Do you want to get 80% of the up-side or 40% of the down-side, or do you want 110% of the up-side with 110% of the down-side?

Q. Somebody walks into your office, they are a professional but they are in the early stages of their career. What is the single most important piece of advice you give them?
A. Today, that answer would be that things aren't like they were 10 years ago where it was about buying and holding forever. It has now become time to do your home work, but for my clients I am the one doing the homework. So if the market makes sense, we will just keep on keeping on; if it makes sense to change, that's what we are going to do. But we are not here for trading. We are still about long-term investing, but we are always looking for better ways to do it.

Q. What do you see as the greatest challenge facing the industry?
A. It's probably a combination of Bernie Madoff, with three quarts of the Scott Trade commercials, the E*TRADE commercials, and the Schwab commercials that all tell you we are evil.

Q. What frustrates you most about the industry?
A. One thing that comes to mind is there are days when I get down on myself and then my business partner in Chicago will say, "Just think of your competition." The point being that, "Wow, there's an awful lot of guys who don't know very much at all about the business." There are still plenty of guys in the field who don't really know anything, but represent themselves as planners.

Q. Do you think our industry is clearly delineated and understood by clients?
A. No.

Q. If you had a college graduate with a degree in finance asking advice of you in terms of career direction and potential opportunities within the financial services business, what would you tell them?

A. If it was something that they really enjoyed, have them go to an independent firm but one with a lot of advisors, a fair amount of advisors, and that they may need to start their career from a combination of salary and commission. If they think that at age 22, 23, or even at 24 that they can make it on a commission basis or in a fee-based world, I don't think it's going to work.

Q. Do you feel the industry today is overly complicated and the number of products are too few or too many?

A. Probably too many. You've got what? 6,000 mutual funds? But then again, choices are good. I don't think the clients perceive it the same way. They don't know that there are thousands of mutual funds and thousands of ETF's and thousands of variable annuities, etc.

Q. So when you look at the economy that we have enjoyed over the last 2-3 years, how significant do you think this period of time has been if you were to consider a new investor, somebody sort of in their middle years, and then a retiree?

A. Well, I think the new retiree is more scared than a new retiree at any time I have been in the business. That is all psychological. I can remember each year that the leadership of our BD would usually do a call and they would make predictions about what's going to happen. Then at the end of the year, they go over what did happen and what was right and what was wrong. They thought that 2009 was going to be the year where people were going to change advisors and it was the biggest opportunity we had to get new clients. At the end of the year, we come to find out that it never happened. Everybody just froze and stayed

> *"So I spend probably about 50 hours a week working, 40 hours in the business and 10 on the business."*

with whoever they were with already. So it seemed like a lot of advisors have said that the last 24 months have just been awful for getting referrals. For new investors, yes now is a good time to be investing. I sort of look at it from the theory of reversion to the mean: if things had been awful then it's the time to get in. I can't tell you why; I just know that it is. I can't tell you I know when, but I can tell you that it will.

Q. Do you currently run traditional management? Do you run active management or do you use third-party managers?
A. Third party managers, yes.

Q. Have you asked them to change in any way their style of management over the last three years?
A. Yes. We tell our clients that the old way of asset allocation, modern portfolio theory, works in the class room but it doesn't work for human beings, which was illustrated in 2008 when everything correlated to one. Now we want to have managers who are flexible, opportunistic, go anywhere, and not long only.

Q. What does your average work week look like in terms of hours spent and allocation of time to various activities?
A. I first break it down to working on the business as opposed to working in the business. I try to push that to the Fridays and not make appointments that day. I try to divide things up. For example on a day-to-day basis I try to talk to ten different people, whether they are clients or prospects. I come in and I look at red tail everyday and I see, "Okay, here's who I need to call back today." I try to schedule a couple of reviews per day. So I spend probably about 50 hours a week working, 40 hours in the business and 10 on the business.

Q. What would you consider your most successful marketing strategy?
A. We had a great system back in the '90's. I did FSSR, that's Financial Strategies for Successful Retirement and we used to

fill a room with prospects. Every time we put it on we would pick up a half a dozen new clients, but it was backbreaking. I had little kids at home and there would be one to two nights a week of getting home and they were already sleeping. That was brutal. The reason we stopped is it just burned out. We were sending out the mailers and nobody was responding. You can't just throw good money at your back because it costs your money to put the thing on. I would say the biggest mistake I made was I never really did replace it. We are looking at a couple things right now.

Q. So how tough were your first three years as a planner?
A. Whoa boy was that tough. My father was already in the business so he had all our relatives! My friends weren't making any money, some of them were in graduate school, and a lot of them weren't going to listen to what Sheldon Harber had to say. What does he know? It was brutal.

Q. What is your personal view of retirement?
A. If I retired at 62 or 65, I think I would have a heart attack. I am just not one of those people that can walk off into the sunset. It's just not part of my psyche. I started working when I was 13. I can't imagine not working. What I can see is a time coming where I am doing three or four day so called "weekend workday vacations." I am 53 and in the last five years I have really noticed myself saying, "I've got to go to Phoenix; I've got to go to Florida. Just for a weekend would be good enough!" Then this year, in July, I found myself saying for the first time, "Michigan or Canada sounds okay."

Q. What's your strategy with respect to the business as you sort of cut back on your hours as you get older?
A. The latter. The more I mull that over I don't see anything wrong with that. At one time I always thought of it like this: I had to have somebody to be able to groom to be the successor and now I am like, "No I don't. I might end up in a better place by maximizing the value all by myself!"

Q. If you had a chance to talk to Bernie Madoff, what would you tell him?
A. I don't know... just that...you know... whether he knows it or not, he cost me and many others a lot of money.

Q. So if there was one thing you could change in this industry, what would it be?
A. Maybe transparency. Every product should be subjected to a full and fair disclosure of costs without anything being unfair. The client says, "What's the fee?" and the guy says, "One percent." Well that's the advisory fee; it's not the cost. There's such a huge difference and that game is played all the time. I think they are attempting to fix this in the 401K marketplace. There are a lot of guys that get these accounts because they just lie to people.

Q. Any closing comments for potential planners or clients that you might want to share?
A. I think technology has done wonders for our business. I can remember when I was petrified of what technology would do to us. Being able to do proposals and email clients and send a newsletter by mass email, things like that are great.

"We service the hell out of our clients. We really don't market and haven't marketed for many, many years."
Lorraine Hart, Hart Patterson Financial Services LLP

Lorraine has been involved in the financial services business for 31 years. She started her financial career with a company called IDS and then went to work at a bank trust department where she worked for four years. She then joined an independent broker dealer as an independent representative, working with them for 15 years before joining Cambridge. Lorraine and her partner Cheryl Patterson employ seven people. One is a planner in training, another is licensed for insurance, and the others are support staff for the partners. They have an attorney on staff, heading their tax practice. Although she resides within the Hart & Patterson confines, when she is acting as an attorney she is separate from Hart & Patterson. They currently manage greater than $150 million in assets. They are a full-service firm, but they happen to live in an area where there are five colleges so many of their clients are college professors. As a result they have extensive knowledge of TIAA/CREF 403B plans as a specialty.

Q. Was a career in financial planning a childhood ambition for you?
A. Not at all. I went to college and always assumed I would be a teacher. I was a physical education major in college. Afterward, I taught at a private high school in Massachusetts and then went on to graduate school for an M.A. in counseling. Unfortunately once I graduated I couldn't find a job in the school system as a counselor and so I answered an ad that said simply: "Earn $1,400 a month." I had an interview with IDS, which was the forerunner of Ameriprise. The position was described as helping people realize their financial

goals. This was very similar to so many of the qualities that a teacher would have that it really interested me. IDS was unique in our business in that it was the first company to understand the importance of financial planning in dealing with clients. I think they were way ahead of their time from that standpoint.

Q. What is your greatest motivation today for being a financial planner?
A. I joined the business because I get a lot of pleasure out of seeing clients fulfill their dreams like helping families send their kids to college, have a comfortable retirement and retire gracefully. It's extremely rewarding.

Q. When you meet with clients now, what do you see as the greatest challenge in the relationship in terms of meeting their needs and expectations?
A. Helping them stay focused on the long term, and not get caught up in the news of the day, is the biggest challenge.

Q. When addressing a new client in the early stages of their career, what is the single most important piece of advice that you can give them?
A. The single most important piece of advice is to start saving early. Sign up for the 403B plan or the 401K plan. It doesn't matter how much you put away, just start.

Q. When you look out over the last couple years, what do you see as the greatest challenge facing the industry?
A. I think the political and regulatory environment is going to be a tough one for us, and it has a lot to do with politics. Somebody's got to pay for the Bernie Madoff crooks in our business. So, instead of having the regulatory agencies look at themselves and say, "What did we do wrong?" They look at us and say, "What did you do wrong?" That's unfortunate for us and the client. The regulations were in place, but the regulators were asleep at the wheel.

Q. So would that be your single biggest frustration with the industry?

A. I think too much of it comes down to politics and Congress doesn't really understand our business. I am not sure that the Financial Industry Regulatory Authority (FINRA) really understands our business. Most of us in this business are not crooks and I think they forget that.

Q. I think I know the answer to this next question, but if you had a chance to follow a different path, what would it be?

A. I would not. I am really thankful that I accidentally got into this business. Every day is different, every client is different. I don't get bored. I do get anxious, and I can't imagine doing anything other than this.

Q. If you had a college graduate with a finance degree sitting across your desk and they had yet to determine a direction for themselves, what would you tell them in terms of following the same career path that you followed?

A. I would hope they wouldn't lean too heavily towards the finance part. When we look at hiring new reps, we care more about who the person is than whether they have a finance degree. I think anyone can learn our business, but who they are as a person isn't going to change. For someone new, regardless of what they majored in, I would tell them that they are going to have to work really hard, they need to be aware that they are dealing with other peoples' money. They need to have ethics and morals – again, going back to the "do unto others" idea – that is the key. Keeping your word, doing what you say you are going to do, and following through on those kinds of things are the biggest keys to success, not what you learned in college.

> "I am not sure that the Financial Industry Regulatory Authority (FINRA) really understands our business. Most of us in this business are not crooks and I think they forget that."

Q. When you look at the industry as a whole today, do you see it as being overly complicated?

A. I think there are some products that are too complicated. In our practice we try to stay with what we understand and what we know. I don't think it has to be complicated. I think there are some in our industry who think the more complicated it is the better. They like to deal with the technical aspects. We don't do that in our practice. We explain to our clients as best as we can, the products they are going to get involved with and what we see as the challenges they may face. We try to solve those challenges for them. Sometimes we see our peers getting so enmeshed in the technicalities of our business that they can't see the forest through the trees. They forget that the end point is to help their clients have a successful retirement or send their kids to school, not to focus on their proprietary investment process or get bogged down in the minutia.

Q. Given our current economy, what do you say to a new investor, an established middle-aged investor, and a retiree?

A. For a new investor I think our economy offers a huge potential for accumulating money over time. I think for the intermediate, middle-aged investor it's the same thing. We tell our clients to buy, not sell, and then explain to them why. Every time the market goes down we encourage our clients to buy. We have many clients set up in systematic investments, whether it's their company's 401K or 403B, so they are taking advantage of market declines. I think the present market represents a great opportunity for clients in all stages of life, even retirees, because they still have a percentage of their assets invested in equities. I think everybody can benefit from equities, no matter what their age.

Q. Very briefly, what sort of investment strategies or portfolio management strategies do you offer?

A. We do not do any in-house portfolio management. We use third-party managers. Primarily we deal with SEI and we have worked with them for the last 12 years. Our job is to manage our client's behavior, and we leave the investment management to the experts. We don't have time to do both of those things because each one is a full-time job.

Q. When you are running a third-party money management system, who guides who in terms of a change in a client's attitude towards their money? Do they simply run model portfolios and then you choose moderate, aggressive, or conservative?

A. If the client's objectives are changing, then we would move them into a more aggressive or less aggressive portfolio. Conversation is certainly an aspect of what we do, but we don't let our clients dictate to us what's happening on a day-to-day basis. If we had done that last year we would have transferred all of our clients assets to cash and we didn't do that. We talk to them about risk, we try to find out what they are afraid of and help them look at other investment options. We don't change a portfolio. We don't move it into a less aggressive position unless we feel something catastrophic has happened in their circumstances or maybe they are getting close to retirement, in which case we'd want to dial down the aggressiveness of their portfolio.

Q. What do you consider your most successful marketing strategy?

A. We service the hell out of our clients. We really don't market and haven't marketed for many, many years. The only marketing we've done is sponsor NPR. We have a mention during "Morning Edition" and then in the afternoon, during the show "All Things Considered." We live in a well-educated and progressive area. People hear our names on public radio and thank us for supporting them. That's been our only marketing. We just treat our own clients as well as we possibly can, and do as much for them as we possibly can. We believe they will refer their friends and family to us and that's pretty much how our business has grown.

Q. Cast your mind back: How tough would you say the first three years of being a financial planner were?

A. Sometimes people will ask me: "How has it been? You have been in this business a long time?" Part of the success of being in the business a long time is outlasting the competition. I think a lot of people give up because there will be lean years, and you just have to be okay with that. We do the same thing we tell our clients to do, we cut back on our expenses, and we work harder. The first few years can be tough, but you've just got to keep persevering and if you are serious about being successful in the business, it will eventually happen.

Q. How do you see retirement for yourself?

A. For me, retirement is being out of the business, because I just worry too much. I couldn't be semi-retired. There are too many things you have to stay current on for the client's benefit. I don't want to be 75 and still going to a national sales conference. I want to be retired. I don't want to have to worry about those kinds of things, because in fairness to my clients, they need their planner to give them their full-time attention.

Q. What are your expectations of the firm after you retire?

A. I don't know whether the existing staff could offer enough money to buy us out. We met with a company out in Washington state a year or two ago. They buy practices, but try to keep the present employees in the office, because obviously they are the ones with the client relationships. I think that may end up being our solution. We have been planners not only for our clients, but planners for our business for a long time. We always look at what are the things we need to be considering five years down the road or seven years down the road. That's part of what we are thinking about now.

Q. If you had a chance to talk to Bernie Madoff, what would you tell him?

A. I would tell him that he should be incredibly ashamed of himself. Whether it's Bernie Madoff or a priest or a teacher or anybody else who betrays the trust of the people they are working with, I think that's absolutely the most despicable thing anybody can do.

Q. If there was one thing you could change about the industry, what would it be?
A. I think the industry is too segmented. I really feel like the planning part of the industry works pretty well, but the brokerage companies need to get back to reality and recognize that their main responsibility is to their clients. It is not to make millions of dollars for the brokerage firm at the expense of the client. Wall Street firms have forgotten this and we are all paying the price for their greed. If I could change anything, it would be that.

Q. Any last comments you would offer to potential clients looking for a new planner?
A. When we meet with a new client one of the things I tell them is that choosing and working with a planner is a lot like a marriage. The dating part is easy, it's the next 30 years you have to worry about. I think trust plays such a big role in our relationship with our clients both in starting the relationship and maintaining it. So if they are comfortable with the person they are talking to, I think that says a lot more than some of the more mundane questions that people sometimes ask. From the standpoint of someone getting into this business, I would say to them, make sure you don't ever do anything that you wouldn't want somebody to do to you. Your word and your reputation are your most important assets.

"If you pick up a starving dog and make him prosperous, he will not bite you. This is the principal difference between a dog and a man."

-Mark Twain

"The greatest challenge is trying to make my clients understand that I am not the silver bullet to solve all of their problems."
Lisa Heath, Financial Partners of Louisiana, LLC

Lisa has worked as a financial planner since 1988. Exposed to the world of financial planning at an early age, Lisa's father started working for Equitable in 1972. In college she worked as a "girl Friday" for a New York Life agent for a couple of years, thus began her long association with the business. Lisa is now a managing partner in Financial Partners of Louisiana. She has 2 full-time employees and assistants who run the day-to-day operations. Lisa's firm is closely allied to a group of five other licensed partners, all are CPA's who sit in on important meetings with clients to work through specific issues. Working so closely within a group having mutual influence has worked well for the firm's clients and partners.

Q. Was a career as a financial planner part of your strategy when you finished high school?

A. No, I actually wanted to be a speech and hearing pathologist. I was very competitive public speaking, successful in extemporaneous speaking and oratory and cross-examination debate with the National Forensic League. Because I was good at speaking, I thought, I would like to be a speech and hearing therapist. Unfortunately, I was not very good at that because I couldn't take the realities of that type of job, dealing with troubled kids. It was too emotional, so I switched my major to finance because I knew I was really good with numbers.

Q. What is your greatest motivation for staying in the business, for continuing to pursue this career?

A. Honestly – I like what I do, I am good at it, and most importantly it is never boring. Those were my criteria, I had to like what I do and be good at it. The funny thing about these studies is that show if you do something that you have an aptitude for, you end up usually really liking your life's work. So I was always really good at numbers and very organized and that just is a good fit for the technical side of financial planning. I am really, truly fascinated by people. I am very interested in knowing their story, because they are never boring and it's never the same thing, the same issues, or the same cast of characters. That's why I am just really lucky that I found this, but it wasn't like I said, "Oh, I want to be a financial planner to make the world a better place." That's really not it. I am motivated to stay in the industry because I am good at it, I like it, it's never boring, and I get paid for it, and quite frankly paid very well for the effort that I put out.

> *"If you take people under your wing as clients, you have to be accountable to them."*

Q. When you meet with clients, what would you consider to be the greatest challenge in meeting their needs?
A. The greatest challenge is trying to make them understand that I am not their silver bullet that is going to solve all of their problems. I think that when people are finally driven to a financial planner, they have issues or worries and think that if they just come here everything is going to be fixed. That's probably my greatest challenge. The second challenge would be that it's very difficult to get them to understand that active participation is required on their part. They can't abdicate all of the decision making and responsibilities. The greatest challenge is having them understand that. Coming here is a great thing for them, but it's not going to solve all their problems.

Q. If someone walks in your office, they have a college degree and are about to begin their own career, what's the single most important piece of advice that you can give them?

A. I always tell them to save, save, save. Save early and save at every opportunity you have.

Q. What do you see as the greatest challenge facing the industry?

A. Lack of confidence in our government, in our markets, in our advisor systems, a lack of confidence in advisors that they can do the right thing for the client.

Q. So what frustrates you the most about the industry?

A. I don't really think there's anything that's really frustrating. I think I have just adopted the attitude of, "Okay, there are rules and instead of getting frustrated, I just need figure out how to use those rules to get what my client needs." So it's more about being willing to be flexible and work around the rules.

Q. So would you consider taking a different path? Do you have any regrets about this path being the path you ultimately chose to follow?

A. No, I have a couple of other degrees, I have a degree in education with part of a master's in special education, so I actually tried to take another path! There was a higher power guiding my footsteps along this road of life. I was doing testing with gifted and talented kids, as well as doing special education for a full semester. My husband got a job here in town and when I moved back, my father said, "Well, you could teach, but you would have to finish your master's and get your certification, or you could come to work with me. Why don't you just come work with me?" I did that for a year and said, "Okay, well this is the money that I could have made as a teacher versus this is the money I am making in the free time I have." After about three years I stopped comparing; there was no going back to teaching.

Q. If somebody presented themselves to you today and they had a finance degree and they were looking for advice on a career, what would you tell them?

A. I would tell them that they are really lucky that they have a finance degree because now they have a great deal of flexibility in how they can work to earn a living. If they really want to do investments or be a planner, I usually say, "Great you are 23 years old, you have a good mind, you need to go to work for a large company like Merrill-Lynch, to learn the back office operations, how markets work, what the procedures are. You need to have some years of life experience under your belt." If they want to manage money for clients, I say, "That's great. You need to learn all about money management systems and the other part of it is you need to be a little bit older because no one is going to give you a million bucks at 23 years old to manage. Although you might be perfectly capable of managing it and know the science part of investments and planning, you don't know the art part of it and you are not going to know that until you have some life experience under your belt." A lot of times I will say, "Go and get your master's and find out what it is you really love about finance. It may be the risk management side. It may be just doing all the analytics of companies. Starting out with a financial planning degree is great; what about it in that industry do you really like?"

Q. When you look at the industry through the 1980's and 1990's and where we are today, do you see it as being overly complicated with respect to both product and in terms of meeting client expectations?

A. I wouldn't say it's complicated; I think it's cluttered in terms of products and alternatives for meeting some of the clients' goals. Anything that is as involved as high finance is going to be complicated, but that's not what I do. So, no I don't think it is too complicated at my level.

Q. When you are talking to three people, somebody that's just kicking off their career, somebody that's established but about 15 to 20 years from retirement, and somebody that's retired, how significant to each of them do you believe this current economy is?

A. In the big picture, the day-to-day economy is really not that game changing in the sense that the older clients have seen probably so much more than we will ever see. I have a guy whom I really respect. He is 87 and he has done very well for himself. He is trained as an attorney, but has always made his life in the oil and gas business. We were moaning and groaning about all this hoo ha, and he said, "You know, we survived World War II, we survived the Korean War, we survived the oil embargo, hell, we survived Jimmy Carter! We are going to survive this era too." So the current economy is important, but it's not game changing. Each one of the examples you gave, it's not going to change their game because their game should not be determined by day-to-day changes in markets, things that you have no control over.

Q. Have you changed your approach to portfolio management in the last three years, in consequence of the ups and downs we have lived through?

A. Not changed in portfolio management, we have still stuck with managed money and hiring experts on that. I think what has changed more is we are spending a lot more time with clients trying to understand how their gut has changed, how their risk tolerance has changed, and if it has changed significantly for a variety of reasons, not just market-driven reasons. We will get more conservative in their portfolio, but we are a fairly conservative firm and we believe in moderation in all things.

Q. What does your average work week look like in terms of hours committed to the task and flexibility?

A. I usually get to the office about 9:00 a.m. I typically don't leave the office for lunch; I get a lot of stuff done over that hour, between 12:00, 12:30, 1:00 p.m. I usually leave at 4:30

or 5:00 p.m. It depends on what time of year it is. I would say I spend probably two or three hours every day directly communicating with clients, either by phone or face to face, maybe another hour or two is spent emailing, doing some directing and a little service work, another hour or two might be spent interacting with my staff, if they have questions, or with my partners.

Q. What would you consider to be the most successful marketing strategy you have employed?

A. I think the best marketing activity we have is just sitting down and talking to clients, being truly interested. I am good at managing the clients. I am good at listening and being truly interested in them as people. That's probably my biggest marketing strategy, I am fascinated by their stories and their lives, I want to know about their kids and what they do.

Q. How tough were your first three years in this business?

A. They were pretty tough, mostly because it was trying to fit this square peg into a round hole because I was with Equitable and it was a sales organization and it was just not logical. It was a lot of 'sell this just because.' It was very tough and I was very lucky that we didn't count on my income whatsoever for paying the bills, which was huge. The other thing that would have made it tough is the Monday night sales calls, everybody shows up at the office on Monday night and you make phone calls. My father was really great, he said, "Lisa, let me just tell you, you don't have to work at night, you don't have to work weekends, and you don't have to work with people you don't like. As long as you take care of the clients that you do have – you will never have to look for clients." So it was very tough trying to build your business for the first three years.

Q. When you look inward, what is your view of retirement?

A. It is morphing every year as I speak to clients who are in their 70's and still work every now and then because they love what they do. I see myself more doing that, I am never the type that just sits around and does nothing. I would say I will probably be "working" well into my 70's. How much work I do every week and where it is done every week is subject to change. I may start coming in three days a week. If my husband "retires" and we move back to the mountains where he grew up (North Alabama), I could see us having a house and staying there maybe two or three weeks a month and then coming down here and working a week and meeting my clients.

Q. What would be your expectation of the firm when you retire?
A. Either way it would continue, whether I phase out over a period of 10 to 15 years, or I quit cold turkey after 10 years. I need to work for at least 10 more years. My expectation of the firm is that it wouldn't miss a beat. We are in the process of grooming my replacement. She is halfway through her CFP, has got a lot of retail experience, and she is very good with people.

Q. If you had a chance to sit down with Mr. Madoff, what would you tell him?
A. I would pass. I have no interest in speaking to him. There is good and evil in every single person and some people, no matter what you do, no matter what you say, will choose the evil in their personality. I say evil in the sense of doing something that they know is not right and is harmful to others. Frankly, there's nothing I can say or do that will change human nature. My grandmother always said, "When you wrestle with pigs, you are going to get dirty. When you lay down with dogs, you are going to get fleas." Those clichés are around for a reason.

Q. Is there anything else you would want to add to this that you feel is pertinent and relevant?
A. Well, the only thing I would say – and this would be not just

for planners, but for people out there who are looking for meaning and something to do with their lives, you just have to figure out what is important to you. You've got to stick to that, you have to be accountable. If you take people under your wing as clients, you have to be accountable to them. You have to find balance and you have to balance work and play. You can't do either one of them all the time, or the other two go out the window.

11

"You just have to do the best you can and start today. If you keep kicking the can down the road, it's just compounding the problem."
Bryan Kelly, The Kelly Group

Bryan has been in the financial planning business for 18 years. He had originally studied computer science and mathematics before completing a BA in economics and finance and a Masters in Financial Planning. His firm is a multi disciplined organization with a significant emphasis in planning, the firm manages approximately $240 million. Bryan is 40 years old, he has 20 employees, ten of whom are strictly planning and the other team members work his tax and accounting area. The firm operates under a BD RIA and is predominantly fee based. This year they will write 40 to 50 true plans and charge for each one, the very deliberate decision being to place a value on the plan and follow the plan in the investment strategy if the client chooses to manage assets through Brian's firm, or, follow the plan independently. But the plan is the backbone of the relationship.

Q. Was a career in financial planning an ambition of yours as a high school student/college student?
A. In high school I was actually in an engineering apprenticeship program going into computer science and mathematics, but in college, my sophomore year, I converted to economics and finance as a double major. When I got out, I knew I wanted to go into the money field. I thought I was going to manage money, but there were no jobs in 1992. Fortunately, I found a place with a $3 million financial firm (fairly large at the time), and just really fell in love with it. I left the small firm I mentioned and went to work for Fidelity Investments. When I left Fidelity, I went into a partnership with someone who is also my uncle. He's a CPA as well as a CFP.

Q. So would you qualify your desire and the vocation of helping clients, helping people through life's challenges as your greatest motivation for being a planner today?

A. Yes. Particularly given the last decade, I really felt like it's a calling when we are sitting down with real families and real households, and providing them good, sound, quality advice, in a time when they really need it. I came from an agricultural community where a lot people weren't as exposed to these opportunities with investments and with financial planning as a whole. I saw farms and small businesses really ravaged by the estate tax and that left an impression upon me. I knew I had a way that I could help people avoid that, and I had a way in which I felt that I could help people accumulate wealth at a better rate than that of traditional savings.

> "...we have bought every portfolio optimizer known to mankind and it was pretty much a waste of money..."

Q. When you meet with clients, what would you qualify as the greatest challenge in meeting their needs/expectations?

A. I think that for right now, people are more fearful, particularly with clients who have never had exposure to a wealth management firm. We don't necessarily work with the $5 million and up kind of households. We are across the board and we have service models that we can work – young professionals just starting out, to people with millions of dollars. We really bring that concierge service that is available with those $10 to $20 million dollar households to the masses in a high quality way. What I have witnessed is that our business grew quite a bit in the difficult market of 2000 through 2002. It drove clients to look for planning, where the plan drives everything and I think that really shows itself during difficult times. People are happy to have someone they feel is on their side and has an open mind with clearly expressed opinions and motives. I am not an idea log in the sense that "broker bad," "planner good." I think there are good people across the spectrum; I just think that many clients have had a bad experience in the brokerage world in many cases. So I guess because we have never promised anything apart from the fact that we would be there to walk every step with them, we have met their expectations.

Q. When they come to you in the early stages of their careers, what's the single most important piece of advice you feel you can give them?

A. Just as in the exercise model with working out, make it hurt. They need to save to a point where it's noticeable. You can do all kinds of fancy analysis, but the basics are to still pay yourself first, try to save 10-20% of your income. You are never going to have enough money for college or retirement. You just have to do the best you can and you have to start today. If you keep kicking the can down the road, it's just compounding the problem.

Q. What do you think is the greatest challenge facing the industry?

A. Wow...That would be, clarity of voice. There are so many diverse agendas from the CFP board of standards, to the FPA. It's so confusing to Joe and Jane Public who an advisor is and what they do. An insurance person could be an advisor, a broker, a lawyer, or an accountant. It's really confusing to the public what makes you different from them. Really we are committed to a process and making sure that we have done our due diligence and can manage realistic expectations, verses going through a simple sales process.

Q. What frustrates you most about the industry today?

A. When somebody calls me a broker I take angst. At the heart of the financial meltdown of 2008, we were holding town hall meetings and answering questions for two or three hours from audiences to help bring some peace of mind to people through community, etc. We are invested in our clients. Particularly frustrating are reactions to lower net worth. For instance, a couple with a hundred thousand dollars in investible assets, or have a half a million dollars in a 401K plan, would tell us about other firms, "They wouldn't help me." It blows my mind because of the compensation metrics out there, that these kinds of accounts are often abandoned.

Q. Casting your mind back, would you still follow the path you did or would you take a different path and why?
A. No, this is what I was put here to do. I am very thankful that I left Fidelity, they are a good firm but they can't compete with us. They can't compete on the quality and the uniqueness of what we deliver. So I really believe I was born to do this. I find people who tend to be really successful in this business tend to be focused on doing some good deed. Financially, I don't sit here and say, "Oh this is how much I make." I am a business person so you have to keep the lights on and take care of your family, but I truly see that there are special people out there and they have a flare for this. We are there to provide a service and cut through the maze of information and the financial pornography that impacts us psychologically every day. This is challenging, it's pretty amazing, you have to be a psychologist, you have to have some financial acumen, and bring all sorts of disciplines under one roof. I think that's what makes it so interesting.

Q. Do you get the sense that the industry is overly complicated at this point in time? Do you think it's just too much for people to contend with?
A. That's interesting; I just came back from the Berkshire Hathaway annual meeting in Omaha where they spoke for about six hours answering questions. We are always searching for the silver bullet. For example, alternatives became very hot a year or so ago. We are always looking for something that's not going to go down, provide an excellent rate of return to us, and so on. We as humans are always saying, "I can pick stocks better than so-and-so." But when you really look at it and you break it down looking at business and evaluating

cash flows, it comes down to earning money, retained earnings, and simple business practices. I think we do complicate it too much. It's often about the show. It's about the sizzle versus the steak.

Q. So with that said, in the realm of our current economy and everything that's going on in the world around us, how significant is the current economy to a new investor, an established investor, and a retiree in your mind with the degree of uncertainty that we currently are seeing?

A. Well, I heard a long time ago this statement that the bear argument is always the most intellectual. I think it is very easy right now to put together a thesis that's showing a pretty bad situation. While I have faith in the system, it just doesn't have the same type of sizzle as talking about Greece and the PIGS and blah, blah, blah. I think that it's always been important to have a conservative based plan if you are in your 70's and you need an income stream. You shouldn't be 100% invested in any one asset class. When you are in your 20's and you're saving, that's a different scenario. So I think keeping it very basic, it hasn't really changed a whole lot. I think we are just more sensitive to it. Base it on the plan and follow the plan.

Q. Now, you take custody of assets and you manage portfolios. Are you following a typical modern portfolio theory, allocation, diversification models, risk tolerance matched, or do you do something that's a little more sophisticated?

A. Well, we have bought every portfolio optimizer known to mankind and it was pretty much a waste of money because when you really look at the sensitivity of those optimizers and the input, it's pretty significant. So we are guided a lot more by common sense asset allocation we believe in. Harry Markowitz and William Sharpe won the Nobel prize when I was an undergrad, so that was deep in my undergrad training in economics and my portfolio theory classes at the time, but we probably weren't as ramped up on the Kool Aid as a person may have been studying in 2000. So we do a core methodology, a core allocation, and we will tweak some of those outside parameters based on situations. For example, in the late '90's we allocated money to real estate and in 2006 we sold that position. We've allocated in and out of the jump bond market, but that's on the outer peripheral and that usually doesn't touch more than 20% of the portfolio.

Q. What does your average work week look like just in terms of structure, but also in terms of total hours worked?

A. I tell people that I don't feel like I work a lot and my wife will disagree with that statement, but it's partially work and I just don't realize I am working. I am also heavily involved in my community, which I wasn't early on in my career because I was spending time actually building clients and a business. Now I am really passionate about giving back. I sit on the board of our local community college and a couple other educational institutions. I would say 60 hours a week between volunteer and work would probably be correct.

Q. From the development of your business, what would you consider your most successful marketing strategy?

A. Doing a good job with the work already on my desk. We have spent a lot of money trying different things, such as seminars particularly, but really what it boils down to is staying in business long enough to do good work and be recognized by your clients. That certainly is what sustains and propels your business. This year we had an economic forum we are calling our "Annual Economic Forum" and we had a pretty well known Baltimore area economist speak who was very entertaining. We had 180 people come. We got a lot of good will; we had our county executive, county councilman, and we had a senator come. They are seeing that we are doing this for our community. We are not hard selling but we certainly got business out of that. So I think it depends on what stage you are in as a business. I see us doing more and more types of things like the forum that are not a direct sale, but indirect high impact events.

Q. How tough were the first three years as a planner?
A. I loved it. I was coming out of school, I was 21 years old and I just had to struggle. I was fortunate because really I was hired as an analyst for a financial planning firm. I loved it so much I would go out at night and bring clients into the firm. As a result, I helped the firm generate a couple hundred thousand dollars in my first year and I didn't even know what that meant. I was just doing it because I believed in it. But I had ethical issues when I started understanding the compensation and things of that nature better. That's why I struggled in gaining my footing and why I went over to Fidelity for awhile. At Fidelity, there were even issues there, and then finally I just said I was going to hang my own shingle out. I did that in 1997. Even though I started with zero clients, it was a lot of fun. The adrenaline was pumping and it felt like I was just doing something that was certainly going to become such that it would be missed if it didn't exist.

Q. So when you look at yourself, what is your view of retirement with regards to you and your family?
A. I will be 40 in October and its interesting: my partner, who is my uncle and who is going through this struggle right now, he said, "Old soldiers never die, they just fade away." I will probably fade away but I will fight you for it. I care about my clients. They are, I hope, lifelong relationships and while I have no issue with people selling their practices, I just don't get selling my client base. I see myself nurturing and grooming a culture that, if I am half as successful, would be like an Eric Schwartz and how he has groomed the Cambridge culture. I think that we will have young people that will come in, and I will still be there working with my clients, but I will become a smaller and smaller piece of the firm.

Q. So if there was anything you could change in this industry, what would it be?

A. I would figure out the compensation challenge. We are committed to the financial planning process and doing planning and advising clients about anything. From whether it's best to lease or buy a car to how to best buy the home, personal residence, etc. But when you look at our revenues, by and large they are coming from portfolio management fees. I would like to know how the services and asset management sides to the business all comes together someday.

Q. Do you feel that the current licensing exams are in any way appropriate to the role we serve or the services we provide to clients?

A. I think it's like giving a child a gun. There is no way on God's green earth that I should be advising someone on the ins and outs of their insurance policy, I have no background in insurance. It's too easy to get access to the industry and a complex issue. You can pass the Series 6 or 7 exams and the Series 66, or worse yet there's been a huge movement in RIA industry and they are Series 65 only. I think the CFP is a pretty challenging test, but it's easy to get a loaded gun in this industry and go out and create havoc.

Q. Would you have any last comment that I haven't covered or touched on that would be relevant from your experience and you would wish to relate to people considering this as a career path?

A. Well my hope, and I believe that this is going to happen, is that the career path is going to become more and more formal. We have done it here in our small organization in our compensation metrics. We have hired advisors on a predominantly salary basis with some incentive, of course, but we have hired the right people where it doesn't really matter to them. They know we will treat them fairly one way or the other, and I would love to see more and more of that continuing to happen. I do look forward to the future. I think it will be better and I think there's going to be more demand for our services than we could have ever imagined. We are probably not yet fully prepared as an industry for it.

"We've found that you cannot guarantee a rate of return, but you can guarantee great service."

-Tony Ruegero

"The greatest challenge is unfortunately people have a mind divided into two parts, a rational part and an irrational part."
Greg Makowski, CFS Investment Advisory Services, LLC

Greg Makowski started in the industry almost 30 years ago, in 1981, and opened his own company in 1989. Greg went to college for classical music; he was a pianist and was planning on continuing his studies in Austria. He fell in love and was advised by his future father-in-law (the owner of an insurance agency) that he might want to get his insurance license while in college just in case he stayed in New Jersey. He did get it and he did stay. Greg first went to work for the Acacia Group to sell life insurance, and was there a short time before he moved to Mutual Benefit Life. He went on to work for a municipal bond firm in New York. After six months, he realized that selling municipal bonds was not of interest to him, but the financial planning aspect was. He continued to advance and experience other companies until, in a single year, he bought his first house, had his first child, and opened up his company. He was 30. In the interim, Greg had attained the CFP designation and taught the CFP curriculum at Fairleigh Dickinson University. When he opened his company, he did fee-based financial planning but morphed the company into a fee-based investment management firm using third-party asset managers.

Q. Was a career in financial planning a childhood ambition?
A. No. Quite frankly, I came from a blue-collar family that didn't have much money. I didn't find out about financial planning until I graduated from college. I thought, "Oh my God, I am not going to Austria, and I'm going to go work for an insurance company," and then the magical lights went on.

Q. So what is your single biggest motivation for being in the business today?

A. Helping people. You know what's interesting, as you have probably seen, is most people consider money the second most important thing in their life, health being the first, and probably, subconsciously, people consider money more important than their health because they will worry themselves sick or dead over money. I tell my wife that it's really like being a highly paid social worker or psychologist. You help people figure out where they are, where they want to be, how to handle their assets, how to accumulate more assets, how to distribute their assets, how to put their kids through college and how to retire. Some of this stuff that we do, people should have been taught in high school or college. That's the fun we have; we actually teach people everything they should have learned in high school or college. It's really just helping people sleep better and achieve whatever their dreams are. So we are just highly paid social workers.

Q. What is the greatest challenge that you come up against when meeting with clients?

A. The greatest challenge I think is that unfortunately people have a mind and their mind is divided into two parts, a rational part and an irrational part. When the stock market is moving rapidly, either up or down, their irrational mind takes over and they react illogically; they do things that potentially destroys wealth. When everything calms down, their rational mind looks at what they did and they are aghast. Then they are upset with themselves and they live in regret. So they are possessed with this irrational mind that goes from fear to greed, from greed to fear, and they can't think clearly so they react poorly. So it's trying to get them to al-

> *"I am in an industry where I can help lots of people achieve their dreams in life and get paid very well and become their trusted advisor and their best friend."*

ways use us as a sounding board, and we have really trained our clients to do that. When times are difficult they call us and we calm their irrational mind, and then when times are too good, and they are trying to throw money at the market, they call us again and we calm them down some more!

Q. When you have somebody who comes to you that is relatively new to their career, they are young but they've got a solid career ahead of them, what is the single most important piece of advice you offer them?

A. I spend time teaching them the whole concept of the time value of money. If they can spend a thousand dollars a year less on their car lease or in the bars and restaurants, and save the money instead, I show them what compounding that money means to them. I try to help them not worry about what their friends have, to keep their debt low and still have a good life, but keep their debt low and to understand how compounding money works over time. When they see that, it blows their mind. Parents often don't understand it. We see it all the time and I hit my head against a wall. An example is when the kid has two college offers: the college of their dreams at $50,000 a year that isn't an Ivy League, so it's not going to give them that leg up in life, and an offer from a comparable college at $30,000 a year. The kid wants to go to the $50,000 college, so the parents hack their lungs out for this $50,000 college; even though it's not a better education. We sit everyone down and show them the time value of money, $20,000 a year invested for four years. We show them what happens if they give the $20,000 to the student in an account that she doesn't know about. At 55 you are going to give her half a million bucks or more. Would the kid rather have that or this education from their "dream" college that's just like the education from this other college? So it's sitting the kid down, when they get the college offers, to show them the time value of money. It blows their mind because they are never taught this and that's what we should be teaching them in school – how to save a little bit and what that means over time.

Q. So having said that, what would be the greatest challenge facing the industry?

A. There's two parts to the industry: there is our industry in financial planning with an independent firm representing clients and being a fiduciary, and then there's Wall Street. To me it's two separate industries. So I think the underlying basis of the greatest challenge for our industry is to get clients to understand we are not that industry, which is Wall street with their "What's in it for me?" attitude versus our industry, with the "What's in it for us," attitude. I'm eventually hoping that we can get ethics and the fiduciary standard installed throughout the industry so that clients are protected and everyone's interests are aligned. Of course we want to make money, but we also want our clients to make money. People should demand a fiduciary standard from Wall Street and their compensation be tied to "what's in it for us".

Q. Do you see any of the current regulatory or industry bodies having the capacity to steer that dialogue to a satisfactory conclusion?

A. I think they are trying. I think this whole Volker rule, separating hedge funds activities from commercial banks is a start. I think part of the problem is the oil that's flowing through congress – money. Wall Street is going to make sure there's a lot of oil flowing. So until the oil stops flowing into congresses pocket, there's not going to be any substantive changes. So we, on our side, have to support our industry groups to make a voice. We have to keep pushing fiduciary standards and what's in it for all of us, versus what's in it for them. This is going to be a long battle, but I think we are going to see some major changes over the next five or six years.

Q. Along a similar line, what would you qualify as your single biggest frustration?

A. If I was a new advisor, or a client, I would be frustrated because everything has gotten too complicated. There are too many products. There's an inverse this, and an inverse that, and leveraged ETF's, and 12,000 mutual funds, as well as managed accounts and unified managed accounts, and many more contraptions! I think it's too expensive; I think total management fees are too high, because you have money manager fees, trading fees, and then you have the advisor fees. I think the whole convoluted talk of fee versus commissions is really missing the point because sometimes commissions are better than fees. If a person has $25,000 or $50,000 in their account and they want you to help them, I am not sure how you help them. I guess you put them in mutual funds that charge a commission, because you can't manage their money for a fee and expect to meet with them annually. Everything's gotten too complicated, too expensive, and I think there's too much voodoo mathematics with the efficient frontier. You have one chance out of 10,000 of having this portfolio have a black swan event and, lo and behold, we have two events in a decade. So I think there's too much voodoo mathematics going on. It's too complicated, too expensive, and too much mathematics, so people are confused.

> "We also need to build financial literacy in high school as well as college students."

Q. If you had a chance to do something different, would you?
A. Well, I would love to be the conductor of the New York philharmonic, but other than that no. I am in an industry where I can help lots of people achieve their dreams in life and get paid very well and become their trusted advisor and their best friend. I can own my own destiny. If you own your own business, nobody can tell you what to do. It's just the greatest business and the greatest experience in the world.

Q. If you had somebody walk in your office, a college graduate with a degree in finance, what would you tell them?
A. First thing I would tell them is to take some courses in communication. I find very few people know how to communicate effectively. They don't speak well in person, they don't speak

well in public, they don't even learn how to talk in complete, coherent, simple sentences. Many times they talk in jargon so a client doesn't even understand what they're saying. So they need to learn how to take a very complicated idea and to make it very understandable. A lot of these people are too much into analysis and portfolio theory. They might be thrilled at doing that and it may be the perfect place for them, but if they want to build an advisory relationship, they need to be able to talk to people effectively.

Q. Are there other extremes in products that you feel are inappropriate?

A. Well, to me it's even more fundamental than that. I really believe that this whole concept of efficient frontier is part of the voodoo mathematics. What happens is people will give a client this beautiful presentation of the efficient frontier, and tell them how we are going to put them on this frontier. But a lot of that frontier is based on historical or projected returns and standard deviations. So people are relying on computer systems instead of common sense. When you need 6.25% in an emerging market bond fund so that you can be on the efficient frontier, to me, that is a lot of nonsense. Common sense has taken a back seat to computerization and it's going to get worse. My children grew up with computers from infancy, so they are going to rely more and more on them, "Hey, whatever comes out of the black box must be right," as opposed to some common sense thinking. It wasn't too long ago you were listening about how great Ivy League universities were doing with their endowments, and all the magical things they were doing. That's kind of all disappeared because it was a lot of voodoo mathematics. People have to get back to basic blocking and tackling, "How do we reduce costs? How do we best invest our money? Is your goal to "get rich" or "stay rich"? It's really just using common sense and figuring out what the client wants and then building a portfolio that meets that need. None of that requires complicated mathematics.

Q. If you consider three broad categories of investors, the first being a new investor, the second being an established investor, and then lastly a retiree, how significant is this current economy to each?

A. What is interesting is the new investor hasn't gone through the last 10-12 years of no returns on the S&P. However, they have heard all the war stories. The new investor will probably invest pretty conservatively, probably more conservatively than their age dictates, because over the last dozen years they have heard their parents talk about all of their losses. Over the long term, that might hurt them because they are going to take potential returns off the table. It's almost like our parents, hearing from their parents about the depression. They never had real hope for economic success or investing and trusting the markets to behave and create wealth for them. That's the mindset that my children, who are 18 and 20, have heard most of their entire life. It's been "Oh my God! We are in a recession; the markets have crashed again. We have global terrorism."

Now the established investor, the people we are seeing, are absolutely shell-shocked. They are all less wealthy than they thought they were going to be. I think it's almost like a general malaise or depression, or a head-in-the-sand attitude, because a lot of people are just ignoring it. They are not actually doing the numbers and saying, "Well, I either have to work longer or I have to save more money. Otherwise, when I retire, I have to retire on less." There again, we see the fight between fear and greed all the time – "Oh my God, I just missed the 80% run up because I put all my money in cash in 2009. Now what do I do?" It's really a general unhappiness that is pervasive in people.

The retiree is in trouble. If the person retired in '98 or '99, unless he was substantially wealthy, he is dead in the water. He has had two major stock market corrections, but even more importantly his interest that he's been earning on his bonds and CD's has cratered. He went from 6-8% interest, down to 2%. They have no hope. So they are searching for yields; they are pouring money into bonds, and as soon as this bond bubble bursts, they are going to lose more principle, so the retiree is dead in the water. The only retirees that will survive intact are those people that have saved a lot of money, always lived beneath their means and had invested conservatively. We are starting to get some of those clients in. They have survived.

Q. What does your average work week look like?
A. It's probably as bad as everybody's; I work a lot. I am in by 7:30am and I typically leave by 5:30pm. That's usually four days a week because on Friday afternoons I play a little golf. So that's probably 45 hours; I spend another 10-12 hours reading and thinking. I love every minute of my time spent working. It's because this is my vocation and my avocation. I spend a lot of time really thinking about how I can create the next financial symphony for my clients and my business.

Q. So how tough were those first three years?
A. Ridiculously difficult. I did it when I was 22 to 25. I could have done it at 30 to 33, but not 40 to 43, not as a change of career. Until the industry really evolves where there are places for executives to go and do something fun like this, until that evolves, it is a game for young people to start. The way I started, this is how crazy it was back then, I went to the newspaper and I found every baby announcement and called those people up and said, "You just had a baby; congratulations. Have you thought about what will happen if you die? Have you thought about what will happen if you become disabled? Have you thought about how you are going to educate your kids? We need to talk." It was cold calling baby leads.

Q. So what is your personal view of retirement?
A. For myself I can't envision retiring because I'm having too

much fun. My daughter says that after she finishes college and spends some years in a career learning about international finance and marketing, she wants to work with me and take over my business. At that time, I will be about 60 and I think then I will probably want to work less hours. Then for the next 20 to 25 years, I'll just have a great time helping my top clients who are also my best friends. You just don't want to pull the plug because you are having so much fun helping people.

Q. Do you see yourself selling your firm, or with somebody like your daughter coming on, do you see it simply transitioning to the next generation?
A. It's tough. I think I would want to transition it unless our kids all said, "We don't want anything to do with it." If that is the case, we will probably sell it.

Q. Do you believe Bernie Madoff actually had a legitimate business, or do you think he was always a crook?
A. Wow...Bernie Madoff...I think I would want to ask him why did he do it? I just want to ask, "How did you betray your family let alone the investors, but how did you betray your family?" How do you look your kids in the eye? I think he had a legitimate business. The problem probably arose when he turned into a hedge fund strategy and was leveraging that. He blew people up. He was so embarrassed that he wanted to dig his way out of it. He was either so embarrassed or so arrogant. He kept digging deeper and deeper, and he wasn't smart enough to get out.

Q. So if there was one thing you were able to pinpoint and influence and change in the industry, what would it be?
A. Well it's something that can't be changed, which is people's thinking. People in the industry and in corporate America need to have their assets and income tied to their decisions, and to suffer or benefit from the consequences of those decisions. This way, with the hedge fund manager, if he blows

it, he can't keep his $100M paycheck. His assets have to stay in the fund for rolling 5 years, or rolling 7 years, so his assets get blown up too. I think in corporate America, the top executives' incomes have to be tied to either real shareholder performance or some other kind of metric. I think that brokers are the same; if you sell a bunch of garbage and blow people up, you need to suffer the consequences. Our industry's income and balance sheets need to be tied to the outcome of the advice provided, on the independent side that is the benefit we offer with fee-based investment management. Our income and our assets go down if our performance isn't good. If we don't do the right thing, then we suffer too. We need to tie our outcome to our client's outcome.

Q. Is there any last comment that you feel would be pertinent to this project that I haven't touched on?
A. We need to attract more people that do good and then they will do well. We also need to build a career path for them. It really is our entire industry. We also need to build financial literacy in high school as well as college students. If we can do that, then we can have a generation of financially smart people that can ask the right questions of us and of our congressman. That is what it is going to take.

"Financial planning and plan design implementation is a puzzle, and it's fluid. I like puzzles."
Chris McGrath and Josh Schwartz, Retirement Plan Advisors

Chris McGrath and Josh Schwartz are 2 of 3 the founding partners of RPA in Chicago. Chris began his career serving public sector retirement plans in 1983, working directly with plan participants as a financial advisor/enroller with one of the nation's leading public sector retirement plan providers, and later as an enroller with the City of Chicago deferred compensation plan. A few years later Chris was promoted to Regional Director and, in due course, Regional Vice President. Joshua began a long history of serving public sector employees and their families after graduating from The University of Chicago in 1987. He began his public sector career as a field enroller and financial educator the same public sector retirement plan provider. He held a number of roles within the firm, including Managing Director and ultimately Regional Director.

In 2000, with another long-term colleague, they founded Retirement Plan Advisors with the goal of offering public sector employers and their employees the option of working with an independent advisor and better managing an important retirement asset.

RPA has built itself around the group retirement plan market with public sector focus and today manages over $1.8 Billion in assets, employs 17 people directly and has 63 independent representatives in their organization. RPA was founded in 2000 following a restructuring in the firm the founding partners had previously worked for.

Q. Was a career as a financial planner in the financial industry a childhood ambition for either of you?

Josh

The answer is no. I thought I was going to be a lawyer, growing up Jewish in New York you thought you would grow up, become a lawyer, and make a lot of money

Chris

I thought I was going to be a special ed teacher, I have a Bachelor's in Education with a Special Ed certificate. My mom was a teacher and I actually taught school for almost a year.

Q. How did you each find yourselves in the financial services industry?

Chris

Reality overcame altruism. I figured out teachers didn't make a lot of money. Why it took that long to dawn on me, I don't know. I was clouded by this vision I had. I was out with some friends and one of the guys was driving a nice car and next month he was driving another nice car, and I said to him "What is it you do ?, is it legal?, and could I do it?" And he said, "I sell deferred compensation plans for Nationwide." Six months later I was working for him as a rep.

Josh

I was playing with the idea of majoring in philosophy and actually getting a PhD in philosophy and becoming a University professor, but my senior year of college I realized just how hard the graduate students were working and I wasn't ready to work that hard so I just started looking for a job. I always liked money and was interested in money. I saw an ad for a management training position at First Investors Corporation, I interviewed and they hired me. The job was basically to cold call and sell mutual funds out of commission and learn the business. I had a manager who was a very good sales trainer. He taught me how to sell, and I am not shy, so I put those things together. At the time, a friend of mine was working with Chris who was already at Nationwide. There was an opening and they referred me.

Chris

I was a manager at this time; I could hire people. Josh had one of the best answers – it's cliché now, but at the time one of my standard interview questions was, "Where do you see yourself in five years?" And Josh said, "Well, after you are promoted, I see myself in your position." I just laughed out loud because it was clever and funny; it was perfect attitude for a sales rep. At that point I said, "Okay, you want to work for us? Here's the gig."

Q. What is your greatest motivation for staying in the business?
Josh

Three things: I really like creative challenge. Financial planning, plan design implementation, is a puzzle and it's fluid. I like puzzles. So there's a puzzle component that I just enjoy personally. I do like helping people and I like running my own business. There's an entrepreneurial component, a self-directing component, and it's an industry that allows for that in ways that a day job doesn't.

Chris

It's partially mercenary and partially inertia. I am 52 and running your own shop is a blast and early on my two partners and I said, "Well, we started this. Now let's build a company and surround ourselves with people we like to work with and let's treat them the way we like to be treated," because we had been treated both well and poorly during our days as corporate employees. We knew we could attract, train and retain producers because we had all done it successfully. I'm not saying it's easy; we just know how to do it. Eleven years later we have largely accomplished that. We work with people we like, we are doing good work for our clients in the financial services industry, we are making money, and we are running our own firm. Plus, we are having fun – we call it the "F" factor – we are having fun.

Chris

Additionally, the three of us respect our relative lifestyle positions, our relative positions in our career. It's cool. It's comfortable – although not to be confused with easy.

Q. What do you see as the greatest challenge in meeting a client's needs?

Chris

Advice; at the group plan level and at the participant level. I said advice pertaining to both the employer and the client level, participant level. Most providers in this space are reluctant to or simply will not provide investment advice. That's the niche that we occupy. Not only are we not afraid to do it, we embrace it. That's a value add for the clients. As market volatility continues, and individual account balances grow, the stakes are higher and our clients need and want investment help and advice.

Josh

We have to get to the Work site, work time, group informational meetings with the employer support. We can get their attention; the issue is advice. We say to them, "We can solve it; we just need you to help a little. You need us to come on site – depending on the size of the entity – annually, semi-annually, quarterly, monthly, even weekly. If there's 30,000 employees in a group, we will have two full time people running around to come on site to provide educational meetings and then opportunities for your employees to meet one on one for retirement counseling. When we get their attention, they say, "That makes sense," and we become part of the fabric of the workplace.

Q. So when you do find yourself in front of an investor, a new investor, an individual, what is the most important piece of advice you offer them?

Josh

Save money, pick a good allocation, and don't make changes without talking to me.

Chris

Save money pre-tax. Allow us to help you pick a good allocation and then see us before you make any changes.

Q. What do you see as the greatest challenge facing the industry?

Chris

The focus of regulation –We have to jump through almost as many hoops as big firms do and the expense of regulation is driving small independents out of the business or driving them to consolidate, and I believe small independents add value to the consumer in terms of choice and personal service.

Josh

This is a perfect example: look at the insurance side, the Variable Annuity. There are all these suitability issues from FINRA on selling a VA, but there are no hurdles on the product company manufacturing the VA. So the lack of consistency across the industry and how regulation is implemented and applied creates a significant disconnect.

Chris

It makes tough for the good guys to make money. The Bad Guys will always be bad guys; it just makes it tough for the good guys.

Josh

And it makes the terrain very difficult for the individual investor. The individual investor isn't really getting apples to apples protection or transparency.

Q. If you guys had a chance to follow a different path, would you?

Josh

I wonder about that sometimes. Private equity, perhaps? I really am happy with what I do. Frustration and difficulty are natural components of all work and endeavors. I wouldn't have done things differently; I wouldn't choose a different vocation.

Chris

Ditto – I have been very happy with what this business has provided me and my family.

Q. Do you think that entrepreneurial thinking is an intricate part of your success, or do you think it was the training you received?

Chris

I would say for me, both. It was the right time, right place. It was my years with Nationwide that made me confident in the business model. I figured we could duplicate that model.

Josh

That division of Nationwide was very entrepreneurial. Everybody was on commission.

Q. If you sat with a college graduate looking across the spectrum of financial services, what advice would you give them?

Chris

I have had that experience. I have had friends ask me to talk to their college age children and I have discouraged them from entering our business, I think it's crowded. I think the barriers to entry are relatively low.

Josh

But the barriers to success are high.

Chris

Yes. And the fall-out rate is enormous. I paint a very realistic picture: You won't make any money for awhile, you won't make good money for a long while, but if you can hang in, ten years from now you will start to make some serious money. I think that's a long horizon for somebody who is 22.

Josh

I don't so much discourage that with the people I talk to. I tell them it is first and foremost asset gathering. You need to be able to get in front of people who have money and have them let you manage it. That's what it is first and foremost.

Q. So what does your average work week look like?

Josh

I work a lot. A combination of a real interest in politics, a real interest in participating in the community, and young kids and a big mortgage and personal ambition. I am the president of the board for my kids school. I have been on finance committees for several election campaigns. I put in a full week here. I am a busy man. I would say 60 hours a week because that's six ten hour days. How do you measure the time from 9:00 to 10:30 when I am doing stuff?

Chris

There's overlap and that's why you don't get push back. If you are at a community meeting talking politics, part of it is satisfying your local community involvement itch and some of it I can see when you connect the dots where we would benefit from it.

Josh

Absolutely.

Chris

Exactly. So there's that and part of the fact that we've been together and trust each other we tend to let the other guy run with stuff.

Josh

Right. The 60 hours wasn't all RPA. It was RPA and all total.

Chris

I certainly have – but I am dialing it down. I certainly work 45-50 hours. Because we run our own business, even on days off we are still communicating with each other. We are rarely completely out. We are either taking 10 minute phone calls here or there, or returning 8-10 emails a day to reps or partners. We joke that when we didn't have any clients it seemed to be a lot easier.

Q. What has been the most successful marketing strategy for RPA?

Chris

Personal relationships. Face-to-face personal relationships. Josh and Jim are road warriors. It's got inertia now, but initially it was Josh and Jim knocking on doors – Josh and Jim and a handful of our reps. And because we have done this all our careers, and we are passionate about it, that comes across. You talk to any one of us, or our reps for that matter,

and you'll get the sense that we have done it for a long time at a high level and we are very committed to our message.
Josh
And we are not publicly traded. I do not need to grow 20% a year. Nationwide, Great West, our competition, they have billions and they need billions more every year. We have a 1% market share, maybe less, or a fraction. We could double and still only be a fraction. I don't care if 80 people say no to me out of 100; if I got 20 yes' out of a hundred I would be thrilled. We only want to talk to the people who understand we add value. If you want the cheapest provider, you should hire somebody else.

Q. How tough were the first three years as a financial planner?
Josh
I started out in the phone book. I would call on Monday to schedule appointments, I delivered pizzas on Friday, Saturday, and Sunday nights to make ends meet.

Q. And when you started RPA, how difficult was it?
Josh
Really hard, especially the first 2-3 years. Chris:Brutal. We directed most of the of commission and fee revenue to our reps so they could make a living and stick with us, and we were depleting our personal savings at the same time to pay for legal fees on their behalf and start up expenses for the firm.

Q. What is your expectation of the firm when you retire?
Josh
I could see RPA becoming institutionalized where it becomes a partnership where people get bought out in stages or not necessarily completely bought out, where then the buyout depth becomes not a huge deal where you have to insure it or whatever. We bring in a couple of people and – you know, Chris and Jim are phasing out, but there will be different stages than that, that there's time to add partners as found-

ing partners and it gets big enough, that middle level of the pyramid, to transition to a – you know, the way a law firm has eight partners and 70 associates and staff and it becomes sustainable.

Josh
I would say that's the goal, but building a sustainable entity, we also believe adds value – increases the valuation, that institutionalization of a practice. There could be a merger with a similar sized firm where it's understood – you look at 18 years from now there could be guys just like us but 10 years younger and it's a merger with the understanding that in that merger is a three year trajectory for Chris and Jim and Josh to be completely out. We are not closed off to everything.

Chris
Yes, I was about to say we are open for anything, but the plan is to have the company continue its growth so that it can support partners stepping back, but we don't envision partners ever stepping completely out.

Q. If there was one thing in the industry you could change, what would it be?

Josh
It'd have to be the regulation.

Chris
I don't know how I would change it.

Josh
That's an excellent observation. We don't know what the right answer is, but the way it is currently regulated –

Chris
Seems the application of the regs is sporadic and not predictable.

Josh
And not consistent across segments. The separation investment advice, securities for commission, and insurance – the biggest problem is the separation of insurance. If in the insurance world, fixed indexed annuities had to live under the

same transparency and disclosure requirements and if they were uniform across all the playing fields, it would allow for simplification.

Chris

I agree. Given the same information in two different formats to two different regulators on two different schedules and it's expensive to have competent people that do that. To be compliant is righteous, but it's also onerous.

Josh

The insurance lobby is incredibly powerful and successful in maintaining state jurisdiction over the insurance industry, which is why there are no federal rules for insurance.

Chris

Surely the insurance lobby is very powerful and creates a disconnect for consumers.

Josh

I would say all players share culpability in the system.

Q. Which of the levels of regulation do you feel is most appropriate and how would you necessarily try to enact that over the other segments of the industry?

Josh

I would start again with a single federal agency that covered commission sales, RIA, and insurance, and that doesn't mean that you don't have certain divisions within it, but the licensing, the disclosure – They need to simplify.

Chris

Exactly. It currently isn't effective – can you say Bernie Madoff? Once every couple of years the Good Guys basically shut down operations for a few days to prove to the regulators that they are good guys. I am all for regulation – that's fine. That's great. I applaud it. But make it consistent and provide uniform across all product lines.

Q. Do you have any last comment or advice to somebody considering this as a career?

Chris

If you have no other source of support, it will be difficult to stay long enough to make a living.

Josh
And again, we are talking in the independent channel in the financial planning world. I would say you have to have a real desire, a desire to work with people and a willingness and an ability to listen to them.

Chris
Right – talk less, listen more.

Josh
Clients will tell you what they want or need; just listen to what they are saying.

"It is not the man who has too little, but the man who craves more, who is poor."

-Anonymous

"The cost of delay is perilously high, or as Albert Einstein once declared 'compound interest to be the most powerful force in the universe.'"
Harris Nydick, CFS Investment Advisory Services, LLC

Harris has been in the business for twenty six years. He was approached by a friend who was starting a business in the new area of financial planning, instead of doing one thing for 500 people, they were going to try to solve a whole bunch of these financial problems for a select few, and specialize in really solving their problems. So with this goal in mind, Harris became one of the first financial planners for New York City's largest independent life insurance agency, and stayed there for five years. Today the firm he manages with his partner, manages somewhere in the neighborhood of $600 million worth of assets. They operate a tight organization with two full-time staff up front, an office manager and a secretary, otherwise known as the Director of First Impressions. They deal with high net worth individuals and many retirement plans. They have a clear goal to continue to grow the firm and push toward a billion dollars in AUM in the next three to five years. A graduate of Syracuse University, Harris has a dual degree from The Whitman School of Management and The Newhouse School of Public Communications.

Q. Was a career in financial planning a childhood ambition of yours?
A. Absolutely not. It was the furthest thing from my mind. I went into college believing I was going to go into the communications business. I specifically positioned myself to go to college at one of the premier communication schools in the country and found myself at Syracuse University. I wasn't even half way through college when the notion of learning business was interesting to me. It wasn't until I was a se-

nior in college that I seriously considered financial planning, but you have to understand in 1983 and 1984, no one knew what the word "Reebok" meant, no one knew what the word "Yuppie" meant, no one knew what the phrase "financial planning" meant. Within a year, everyone knew what these things meant. I was at the crest of the wave of a new profession. Even though the idea of CFP was out there – the notion of the financial planning as a career, most people who were financial planners were just using that as a mask to sell product. I was part of what I believe to be the first generation of people that were born into this business to solve problems, not to sell product.

Q. What would you now consider your greatest motivation for being a planner?

A. Well, my greatest motivation for being a planner is that I can be introduced into a situation with a family business or a high net worth individual, and they are better off after I have met with them. If I can take someone's situation and I can help build bridges from here to tomorrow for them, take their dreams, turn it into financialese, create a financial solution, translate it back into English, present it to them, and have their money work harder and more efficiently than it was working before, then I have truly helped somebody. Everyone's situation is different so every day is different.

Q. When you consider your relationships with your individual clients, what is the greatest challenge in meeting their expectations?

A. Well, I'd have to say the greatest challenge is helping them to shape their expectations. Case in point, when the spring of 2000 came around, the pendulum had swung so ridiculously, I was dealing with people who thought they were going to retire early, and in fact some did retire early. Then of course the rest of 2000-2002 came, and the pendulum swung in the other direction. Then in the fall of 2008, when the great recession hit us and our financial disaster had ensued, those in the 50 to 60 age group were telling me, "Oh no. Now I am going to have to work forever." It wasn't true in 2000 that they were going to retire early, but it was also likely true in 2008 that they weren't going to have to work forever either. I am just fortunate that the piece of advice that I dispensed to almost anyone who would listen to me, came true so fast [about staying the course]. No one thought that the market would come back 75% 14 months later.

Q. When a college graduate comes to you and they have a career path chosen, what would you consider the single most important piece of advice is that you can offer them about staging their lives?

A. The first thing is to start early. We all develop habits; we all have habits in our lives and if you are early in your career you are going to develop financial habits. Like anything else, there are good habits and there are bad habits. Like good habits, they need to be worked on. Bad habits just seem to come, you don't have to go looking for bad habits; they find you. So you need to start good habits early. What that means is you've got to look at your salary as an orange. You have to look at a variety of needs that you may not be considering as glasses. You then have to start thinking about how much juice you are going to squeeze out of that orange into each of the glasses. At some point, if you have kids, you are perhaps going to want to send them to college. At some point you are going to want to retire. Of course, there's the bucket for enjoying your life now and then there's the bucket for if something goes wrong. You have a discussion about doing something; that is better than doing nothing. The cost of delay is perilously high, or as Albert Einstein once declared "compound interest to be the most powerful force in the universe."

> *"I was part of what I believe to be the first generation of people that were born into this business to solve problems, not to sell product."*

Q. What would your considered view be of the greatest challenge facing the industry today?

A. The greatest challenge is that we are really at least two industries. You've got people who are working in wire house environments who are working to the suitability standard. And then you have the RIA community and the rest of the independents working under a fiduciary standard. Consider the issue of fiduciary responsibility when working as an advisor inside a publicly traded company. To whom does your fiduciary responsibility lie? The company. Who does the company's fiduciary responsibility relate to? Where does their responsibility lie? It's their share holders. So if the person who is advising me has a fiduciary responsibility to their share holders, where do I come in the line as the customer? Why would I ever consider that an acceptable relationship, especially when I can go to the guy next door and know that his fiduciary responsibility is to me first, the customer? The customer's interest must come first, ethically and legally. So I think the greatest challenge is the fact that you would think there would be no push back on this simple demand for a standardized fiduciary expectation no matter who is advising. In fact if you look at Goldman Sachs' defense, it is basically this, "Somebody asked us to do something. It was good for the shareholders. Someone else was willing to buy it, but they got pillaged and that's free market. I don't understand what the problem is." That is their defense.

> *"I hope to deliver an investment plan review on a Monday and drop dead on a Tuesday, many, many, years from now."*

It's just one big cauldron. We are all put in the same stew. That's the greatest challenge facing the industry. Realize the argument five years ago was commission versus fees. I think that's irrelevant. Price is only an issue in the absence of perceived value. No buyer asks how much the Bentley costs. No purchaser asks how much the Tiffany ring costs. I think all the clients expect us to get paid as long as you are honest and forthright and you disclose how you are getting paid in each and every situation. Then you've got two adults coming together and agreeing on how the goods and services are going to be acquired and at what price.

Q. So is this boiling cauldron of differences your single biggest frustration with the industry?
A. Interestingly enough it's how the press aids and abets the industry. For example, Barons' just released its annual 100 best financial advisors list. They know the difference between a stockbroker, an investment advisor and a financial planner. But when you look at their list that came out recently, of the 100 best financial advisors, it should have been the 100 best stockbrokers. 90 out of 100 of these "advisors" work for wire house companies. A more truthful list would have been called 100 best stockbrokers. So the press actively promotes the notion that we are all in one industry. A stockbroker is a stockbroker not a financial advisor, but we have no truth in advertising requirements in this industry. So that's what frustrates me most about the industry.

Q. If you had a chance to follow a different path, looking back, would you?
A. Not a chance because the only sacrifices that I feel that I have really made are that at certain times in my career I have sacrificed time with my family to build my business, and other times I have sacrificed economic opportunity so I could spend time with my family. Those are trade-offs I felt were good ideas and I learned from each of those, but I can't imagine doing anything else. When the 2000 thing happened, all my clients called me and said, "Is my money alright?" When the 2008 debacle occurred, all of my clients called me and said, "Are you alright?" I can't begin to tell you what a humbling experience that was. It showed me that I had made not only the right career choice, but I had made the right choice as to the customers I allowed to enter my business.

Q. So if you were presented with a finance graduate considering your chosen career, what words of advice would you give them?

A. I would tell a young graduate two things. First, you should probably work for a large company before you work for a small one, there is an overwhelmingly preponderance in numbers of financial advisory firms of 10 advisors or less. I think you have to work in a big company environment initially, go get that out of your system. Go see what that's about. Go see how you have to basically check your soul at the door when you go to work there and forget about having a life. To most large organizations your personal life is secondary. It's all about what the company needs. And you get paid handsomely for making those kinds of sacrifices, but the emotional toll eventually builds. At some point you want to get married, you want to settle down, you want to have kids. You want to have a life. It's only then that the idea of working in a less stressful environment appeals to you.

Q. Do you believe the industry today is manageable or is it becoming overly complicated in terms of its product offerings?

A. It depends on how you look at the industry. If you look at the industry as product, of course it is overwhelming. But I don't consider myself in the product business; I am in the problem solving business. I've got to tell you, the problems don't change that much. People want to retire and do so in a comfortable manner. If they have kids, they want to educate them. If they have sick or elderly parents, they've got to be responsible for it. What is interesting is the problems don't change. I entered the business right out of college and I remember telling my father about my decision. He seemed pretty concerned because he had laid out his life savings for me to go to a very expensive college and I had three other great job offers from large corporations. I tell him about the financial planning. "What's that?" I said, "Well, you know how you get your life insurance from Mike-what's-his-name, and you get your stocks from Jerry, and you get your bonds from Fred? You go to the local bank and every time you open a new account or give them a lot of money, they give you toaster? Well, I am going to do all those things." A look of disgust came upon his face. I don't think he knew what to say to me, but here's what came out of his mouth, "Well son, I really don't know what to say except that Fred, Jerry, and Tom are the three biggest assholes I know. But good luck to you." I am happy to say that my dad is still my best friend and is very proud of my accomplishments.

Q. In your view, when you are talking to your clients, how significant has the last three years been if you are a new investor, an established investor, or a retiree?

A. First let's talk about the new investor. I feel pretty confident that the people, who have been first time investors in the last three years, are going to spend the rest of their lives with a money personality that resembles our grandparents because of what we went through in 2008. It was the closest thing to a depression that we've experienced. In other words, they have a depression mentality. Today's young investor is going to be overly cautious, very conservative. He or she will perhaps leave thousands of dollars on the table over their lifetime. They won't take the appropriate amount of risk, given their age and given their time frame, for their goal whether it is college if you have a newborn, or retirement. I think the new investor pays the highest penalty here, over their lifetime.

Established investors are established in two ways, not just established as investors but established with us. I have already brought them through this mess once before in 2000-2002. I was very fortunate; I had absolutely no push back from my clients. They said, "Harris, you got us through the last one, you'll get us through this one. Do whatever you think is best." The people who were the most nervous and the people who left us, were the people who had come on board to our firm mostly in 2003-2005, in the after math of 2000-2002. I think psychologically what they sensed was, "Wait a minute; this happened to me once before, it's happening once again. I am outta here." But for our established investors, I think it's significant in that between 2000 and 2008, they are all eight or nine years older. Someone who is 30 or 40 is now 50 or 60. So it's important to realize it's caused them to reassess what their true risk profile is because at the end of the day, it's not that we are risk averse, we are loss averse. People say, "Oh, I can handle risk." They just can't handle loss.

As far as a retiree is concerned, for most of my retirees I had predominantly a fixed income strategy. Don't forget; they lose too because interest rates are nearly zero and there's nothing to protect them from that except the solace of knowing that his neighbor probably got fleeced because he stayed in equities a little bit too long.

Q. I wanted to get an opinion from you on thepreponderance of ETFs in recent years, particularly leveraged ETFs and whether or not you feel they are suitable products for all-comers or whether or not there should be limits on their use for the general public?

A. ETFs are very interesting investment instruments and when used properly I think are outstanding investments. I think they are being misused by some and I think the use of leverage is one of the greatest misuses. We are not fans of them. We think that a lot of people don't understand how they really work and that's where we stand. We don't allow any of our clients to participate in leveraged ETFs. If they want to, we just send them down to 1-800-turnmymoneyintodust online brokerage firm and let them lose their money on their own. Now, there are some very interesting ETF ideas that are out there right now that we do embrace. I love the iShare idea of how they have taken municipal bonds and built a ladder for someone else, having already done the heavy lifting.

Q. So from a personal standpoint, what is your average work week look like?
A. I am at work between 9:00 and 9:30 a.m. every day. I am usually here until 6:00 or 6:30 p.m. every day. I see clients and I try to have a personal interaction with clients as opposed to just talking with them over the phone. Built into that with the 401K's don't forget, I am meeting with the trustees on a regular basis reviewing the investments and assisting them with all their fiduciary concerns. I am meeting with participants a couple times a year on education and investments, and I am regularly meeting with my personal clients as well. In terms of flexibility, I will be taking an hour and a half off this afternoon to attend my son's volleyball game. Yesterday morning I took an hour and a half off to take him to a college fair.

Let me tell you this story, one of my favorite stories. I was driving home my son, who was 11 years old at the time, from baseball practice at four o'clock on a Thursday. He said, "Dad, I am going to do what you do when I grow up." I said the only thing I thought I could say at that point, "What do I do? Do you know what I do?" He says, "No. I don't know what you do." I said, "So, help me here. You don't know what I do, but you want to do what I do for a living." He says, "That's right." I said, "Okay, you got me. How did you come to this conclusion?" "You are the only dad who can sit through and watch all the baseball games. You are the only dad who can sit through all the baseball practices. You are the only dad on the team who comes to every practice and every game, and that's what I want to be."

Q. So have you ever done any marketing whatsoever?
A. Strictly word of mouth and through the TPA's and CPA's that we work with; a couple of lawyers, a couple of professionals. But I don't belong to any networking organization and I don't do seminars and I don't cold call. I don't do any of that. It is strictly by referral. Maybe that is what allows us to grow our

business organically. That said, I should have a more organized marketing plan in place.

Q. How tough were your first three years?
A. I was so naïve. Looking back on it, it was tougher than I felt it was at the time. I was young, I wasn't married, and my wife who was my girlfriend at the time, was also very supportive. She was working, we had very low overhead, and success came fairly quickly for me. I partnered up with a guy who had too many clients, and I said, "Give me whoever you want and I will give you 50% of whatever I earn." I said, "I will give you 50% of what they refer, but I own everything after that." And he said, "Okay." So I spent my first six or seven months just toiling, making a living, making my minimums. Somewhere along the eighth or ninth month of doing this, I was referred to a fashion photographer who then referred me to a "Who's Who"of New York City's publishing industry. Next thing you know I was doing work for the editor of US magazine, the stylist of the People magazine, the publisher of Metropolitan Home and, frankly, I never looked back after that. I worked six days a week and Sunday nights. Sunday nights I would plan my entire week. Don't forget this was long before the "do not call" laws were introduced. But I wasn't cold calling people; I was calling my mentors old clients, clients who hadn't heard from him in awhile. So they were kind of warm leads. People weren't hanging up on me; they were receptive. I was willing to give up 50%; that was my tuition for the education I was receiving.

The first four or five years I worked extremely hard. I worked a lot of hours, probably 60 or 70 hours a week. I probably was starting at 6:00 or 7:00 in the morning and not getting done till 10:00 at night. I would eat two breakfasts if I had two different clients at that time of day. I would have two dinners if I had to. I would drive a lot. You know how I justified that? At the end of my first year I calculated that I had driven something like 24,000 miles. I took my income and I divided that into it, and I knew how much money I was making per mile. So the little game I would play with myself when I would have to go on a long drive was that it didn't matter what happened at the meeting, because I knew I was going to make a certain amount of money since that's what it averaged out to.

Q. What is your view of your retirement?
A. I hope to deliver an investment plan review on a Monday and drop dead on a Tuesday, many, many, years from now. My view of retirement is I don't think I will ever stop doing this. I think it's important that we keep all the muscles in our body working, but no muscle is more important than the one in our head. When I sell my business or move on from this position, I will probably take the 10 or 15 people with whom I enjoy my relationship with the most – it will have nothing to do with how much money they manage with me – and just continue to socialize with them and do their financial planning. That's how I see myself retiring, and I will sell the rest. Right now we are too young and we are having too much fun to think about slowing down the growth of our firm.

Q. If you had the chance to talk to Mr. Madoff what would you tell him?
A. I would probably ask the same question that anyone else would. First of all I wouldn't ask why; I understand why. I would probably want to know how. How could you have the capacity to do so much evil? Financial evil is what he perpetrated. It's one thing to be greedy and take money from people's organizations, but when you specifically look at some of the organizations he knowingly took money from, to bankrupt a man like Elie Wiesel and his foundation, to bankrupt all these charitable groups, to bankrupt Hadassah Hospital, to bankrupt Yeshiva University, how could he do this? With a jail sentence of 100+ years, I pray that he remains healthy and lives a long time.

Q. If there was one thing you could change in the industry, what would it be?

A. I don't think we get much choice because change just comes whether we like it or not. It's like the premise of the book by Spencer Johnson, MD, "Who moved My Cheese?" You always have to be willing to move. I think we should have more transparency in the industry in terms of what the actual costs of what investments are and the total costs of retirement plans. I think that the true costs are hidden from the investor.

Q. Are there any last comments that you would want to include in this project for potential planners or even potential clients?

A. Yes, I think you have to love math and you've got to love helping people. You have to embrace the idea that in order to succeed it's not enough to be a good financial planner. You are also going to have to be a good businessman. You are going to have to know how to run a business. It's a pretty wide skill set.

"Everything that I have read in the press says that financial planning is still a very, very strong profession."
Henrietta Nye, Keir Educational Resources (Kier Success)

Henrietta has been with Keir Educational Resources since 1983. She oversees the marketing and production sides of the business. Her claim to fame has been hiring the great people that produce the products or communicate with the customers. An outstanding team makes her job look easy. Henrietta has watched the company expand from only CLU/ChFC® and CPCU® course materials, to the many products Keir offers today. Henrietta has been a member and an officer of many local financial planning organizations. When not in the office, she enjoys paddling a canoe through the wilds of Minnesota or Canada.

Q. As an educator within the financial services industry, what do you see happening in professional education?
A. My interest in the industry, obviously, is to increase the involvement in education so that more people are interested in our products. It is a well known fact that there is tremendous turnover in the insurance industry. With insurance and financial planning, the four year retention is very low. Whether that is due to people not understanding the process, I don't know. For the products that we offer, the turnover is a wonderful part of our business. We can expect a very large number of people to constantly be taking the pre-licensing courses, and then hopefully into the securities licensing and designations.

We are fairly new to the pre-licensing. We have never done any tracking to see what the retention is from pre-licensing to licensing designations. The groups awarding designations can document the number of students who take course one and never come back for course two. Whether it is too time consuming, too difficult, or whether they leave the industry – I can't tell you exactly, but the completion ratio from beginning to end is very, very low. There is at least a 50% drop off from course one to course two. I think it's 50% on to the third course as well and there are eight courses in the process, so it's a very small number that complete.

Q. So if a hundred people go in on that basis, what does that give you, a 12.5% completion rate?
A. That's probably just for those who get into course three or four. I would venture a guess it is lower than that.

Q. In the CFP® courses, does Keir see younger people, do you see a lot of mid-career guys? Is there a general demographic that stands out, or is it just a mix?
A. The CFP board has a research study on this. They will release a report and it shows the vast majority of those who study to achieve their CFP® are in their 30's. They have actual information as to the numbers starting in their 20's and retention through to their 50's.

It is well documented that the vast majority of people in the insurance and financial services industries right now are in their 50's and we have to replace these. We are seeing quite a bit of growth in bachelor's programs for financial planning. Perhaps as people actually major in financial planning, they may have a better idea as to what the career is, what the expectations are, and as you said maybe have more of an emphasis towards the financial planning rather than such a strong sales process. Learning to serve more and have your mind set to help-

> *"...the vast majority of people in the insurance and financial services industries right now are in their 50's and we have to replace them."*

ing people, and helping yourself along the way. I think we may have more successes if they have the background and the knowledge for the career, with more people actually majoring in it. Over the years I have met many insurance agents and financial planners with backgrounds in teaching; I have met several who were music majors, and engineering is very popular for people going into financial planning. It may be the organizational skills and the number interest, but engineers seem to do very well in a second career with financial planning. But what will the future hold for people who actually major in financial planning? I don't know. I think it will be very positive.

Q. You mentioned there were more bachelor courses. Are they offered all across the country?
A. In January 2007 the CFP board required that a CFP® had to have a college degree, any major. Before that regulation was in place many of the universities were starting to offer majors in financial planning where in the past, the school had only offered a certificate program. Planners with a bachelor's degree can participate in a certificate program to earn the CFP®. They can be found all over the country, there are several programs in every state including several online programs. I believe there are 170 universities that are offering certificate programs, and there are about 70 or 75 who offer bachelor's programs specifically to financial planning, and a few of them have a master's program also.

Q. What does a Ph.D. in financial planning involve?
A. Many, many years! These are the people who want to go back and teach financial planning at the university level. As there are more and more bachelor programs, there will be more demand for Ph.D.s on staff.

Q. Do planners see the last three years as having shocked the confidence of the client and they are now struggling to sort of regain a footing?

A. What I hear from conventions and my visits around the country is that the good financial planners have taken advantage of the last two years to increase their communications with their clients and have really seen high retention and a very strong loyalty. Everything that I have read in the press says that financial planning is still a very, very strong profession. It will be one of the top ten professions for the next seven to ten years. People are very concerned, particularly the very high population that is now getting ready to retire. There's so much more information and programs. There are even webinars on the distribution of the investments. Now that you are retiring, you need a financial planner currently more than ever before. How are you going to survive the next 10 to 20 years of retirement? I think there's a lot of optimism and a lot of power in the financial planning practice. Life is totally different; you are not seeing the independents that the baby boomers had living on their own. There's many more boomerang kids going back home, they can't get on their feet. They could start seeking financial planning for themselves and prepare a very, very different future. I think there is lots of opportunity.

Q. Do you see any specific hurdles that the industry is going to have to deal with under the new regulations?

A. Watching it and seeing what the conversation is about, I anticipate there will be more regulation; I just don't know what it is going to be or who is going to take responsibility for it. The next six months are going to be very interesting. I would anticipate more regulation in some form.

Q. Is it your belief that the CFP® designation should be a minimum standard for somebody to hold themselves out as a planner or an advisor?

A. Within the insurance and financial services industry there are many designations. Other well respected designations are the ChFC® and the CLU®. I do think it is very positive for a financial planner to have a designation from the industry.

I am not sure that the public will have more recognition to the CFP®, but I think they recognize letters and that a person has done something beyond the norm to have some letters. I think that due to the CFP® board's advertising, the public recognizes the CFP® a little bit better. I am not sure they know exactly what it is, but I do believe they are checking for CFP® when they select a financial planner. Do I think that's necessary or critical? That depends on the clientele with whom the financial planner is working. If the planners are working with the general public, I think the CFP® might be recognized first. If the clientele are professionals, such as CPAs and attorneys, they might want to look at a ChFC® or CLU®. It depends on your practice and your market.

Q. Is there anything else that you think is a standout situation from your side of the fence, which may be a game changer in the next three to five years, other than a completely new economy?

A. I think that if you talk on the education side, the item to watch is the new recommendation coming out in 2012. That is that any person wanting to become a CFP® will have to complete a course that requires the preparation of a financial plan. The student will have to write a financial plan and make a written and oral presentation of the plan. We don't know what all the regulations of this will be, but that will change the game in 2012. We are encouraging people to complete the CFP in 2011 if possible. I personally feel this new course is a very good move; if you are going to hold yourself out there as a financial planner, you ought to be able to prepare a financial plan. My only concern is the regulations have not been really, clearly adopted and communicated. So I think that in 2012, possibly even 2013, things will be a little unstable just trying to figure out how it will all work, and how the distance learning programs are going to handle this. The end result is going to be very good; there's just going to be a little shake up in those early years. I would also expect more regulation of the industry in the years to come. Get ready for more exams!

"Thousands upon thousands are yearly brought into a state of real poverty by their great anxiety not to be thought poor."

-William Cobbett

16

"It is a tremendous ability to be able to take all of the knowledge and expertise that we have, and be able to provide value to people."
Cheryl Patterson, Hart Patterson Financial Services LLP

Cheryl Patterson grew up in Western Massachusetts. After entering graduate school, Cheryl's thoughts were on owning and operating her own type of exercise or fitness center. She did quite a bit of teaching in grad school and enjoyed that a lot, but really enjoyed the business classes and so she erred toward the financial planning industry. During her employment at Merrill-Lynch, she was introduced to Lorraine Hart by a mutual friend. Cheryl and her partner, Lorraine, started their business together 18 years ago, April Fool's day of 1992. They currently manage greater than $150M of assets.

Q. Your career as a financial planner, was it a childhood ambition?
A. No, not at all. For me, I didn't start thinking about being in the investment world until I was in grad school at the University of Maryland getting my masters in exercise physiology and started taking some business classes. I certainly enjoyed the exercise physiology, I had thought I would be involved with my own fitness center or as a trainer, but was surprised at how much I enjoyed the business classes and one thing led to another. So it wasn't until I was in my early 20's that I decided on a career in the finance world.

Q. So what is your greatest motivation for being a planner today?
A. I am motivated the most by helping our clients, our employees, and the community we live in, be more financially secure. Whatever Lorraine and I can do to that end is what

really gets me up in the morning or keeps me up late at night working. To help our clients have more financial stability in their lives. Our goal is to provide our employees with a great work environment and one we would want to be in as an employee. We feel an obligation and a desire to help the communities that we live in.

Q. And within the client community itself, what do you see as the greatest challenge in meeting a client's expectations?

A. I would have to say that our goal is to exceed client expectations. What I mean by that is they know we are thinking about them all the time. Instead of them having to call us, I am hoping that nine times out of ten, our office is contacting them first and connecting with them. I think our biggest challenge is having our clients inundated by 24-7 sound bytes that are generally negative and having clients able to step back from the media regarding the markets. We want to help people see the very big picture, when so often they are being hit over the head with what is happening this second and having it hyped in the media.

Q. When you have a potential client walk into your office, they are young and well educated, what is the single most important piece of advice that you would give them?

A. I would say that number one you have the benefit of time. That would be the single most important thing. Because you have time, if you start today, you are going to be able to take advantage of a lot of volatility in your lifetime and as an investor, the sooner you take advantage of volatility and make volatility your friend, the better off you are. You need time and money. So if you are socking money away for 30-odd years for your retirement, 40 years in some cases, it's the time you have that's even more important than how much you are starting off with today.

Q. What's the greatest challenge facing the industry today?

A. I think the biggest challenge is the constant 24-7 sound byte that can really get people very uneasy and very nervous and distracted. When I meet with clients, they tell me, "I read this article...I listened to this on the radio..." It's not that we don't want clients informed, that's not at all what I am saying. But it's again being able to put information constantly into perspective for them. I think that is consistently my biggest challenge.

Q. What frustrates you most about the industry as it is today?
A. I really get very frustrated at how defensive our industry is about the fact that we get paid. I really think that is not the position to take. We deserve to be paid, just like any other professional. To make the fee the focus is missing the point. I have said to clients over the years, when I go to the doctor, my first question is not, "How much is this going to cost me?" It's, "I've got a need; can you help me? Do you have the expertise to do that?" The industry has done a terrible job of making the fact that professionals that do what we do, are going to get paid. I find it extremely frustrating that it is the beginning part of many conversations. Although it should absolutely be a part of it, it shouldn't be what we are leading with.

> "I really get very frustrated at how defensive our industry is about the fact that we get paid."

Q. If you had a chance to take a different career path, would you?
A. No. I really feel so fortunate to have chosen this so many years ago. I am thrilled to not only be a planner, but be a business owner and be surrounded by wonderful people that work with us. I am lucky to have a client base of people that I enjoy. Looking back after all of these years, I am very happy that I chose it and stuck with it when it was a very difficult beginning at Merrill-Lynch. I knew I loved the industry and said to myself, "There's got to be a way to do this where

I can also enjoy doing it."

Q. So if you sat down with two college graduates today, one who had a degree in finance, and one who was considering this as a career, what would you tell them?

A. I would strongly recommend that they get affiliated with a firm where they would have industry training. It's terrific that there are these internship programs with these different investment companies. I think the early on training is really important. When I started with Merrill-Lynch, I did not go through their normal training program and I am not saying that's good or bad, it's just what it was. When I look back at what Lorraine's training was through the old IDS which is now Ameriprise, it was significant. Try to intern with a company or get some type of affiliation where you are not just getting your first job. Try to work with a company that is committed to education and training. It's very important.

Q. So when you look at the industry as a whole today, do you see it as being overly complicated and the variety of products too many or too few?

A. I think that it is complicated, but that's why people need you and me and they need somebody that can see all of these moving parts and put it together. I use the example often with new clients that if I bought a new airplane model today that had 200 pieces, I would have an airplane, but it's not together. So I would need to put the thing together to really have the model, the airplane. That often resonates with people. The pieces need to be put together and that is quite honestly so much about what I enjoy regarding this business. We are able to evaluate whether the new strategies or new offerings are appropriate for our clients or not. I strongly recommend that individuals work with somebody to help them through the maze.

Q. So when they come to you and they sit down, depending on whether they are a new investor, they are an established investor, or they are actually a retiree, how do you quantify the last two years to those individuals? How significant have they been to their respective demographic?

A. That's a very good question. The younger clients I say, "You are so fortunate to have lived through this early on in your investing career, to know what the possibilities are of good times and terrible times." I think it is an amazing time for young investors to know how wild the swings can be and how they can come, seemingly, out of left field. Again, I kind of go back to the dollar cost averaging and the investing. For our clients that are accumulating wealth, we definitely concentrate on, "Are you able to sleep at night?" I think we all understand our level of risk when we get pushed off the cliff. It's one thing just to talk about it; it's another thing to live through it. So I think coming back full circle with those discussions with clients, and saying, "Okay, now that we have the benefit of this being behind us, and if this were to happen again tomorrow, are you comfortable with maintaining the allocation you have been? Or, do you think you should become a little more conservative?" It's more those kinds of conversations, really getting them focused on not moving to cash with their 401(k), their 403(b), and what a significant difference that has made. It has been amazing to look at our inception to present returns of our clients. We look at returns since the beginning of this year, to see the different returns between clients that have consistently added to there retirement plans through that period and had the ability to do so, versus those that had a lump sum and couldn't add to it. With retirees we have had the discussion about whether or not we want to be more conservative? I would say that we have not made any major shifts.

It's not like all the sudden we are putting the brakes on here, but maybe I would describe it as fine-tuning those conversations with clients because now they have this experience and have the benefit of looking in the rear view mirror and saying, "What would you do and how would you react if this were to happen again? Should we do anything differently so you have peace of mind and are not up at 3:00am worrying about these things?" Certainly the last two years has been much more significant for retirees than for any other demographic. It comes back to taking reasonable distributions to begin with and having flexibility. In talking with our clients we said, "If you are able to decrease those distributions a little bit during this time period, that is what we would highly recommend." The vast majority of our clients were able to do this, and that was significant. That's how we have managed through those times; it was a very active dialogue with clients.

Q. What does your average work week look like?
A. It's a combination of running the office and all the different aspects of financial planning and steering a ship. We are where we want to be in terms of different tasks and different projects. We are always thinking about what else we can deliver to clients, whether that is fine tuning the system for rebalancing or new information for newsletters or the website. In addition, it is obviously reviewing portfolios constantly. We attend and participate in a lot of meetings to keep up to date with what is going on in the industry. I am meeting with clients three days a week. We typically have Tuesdays as our planning day. It lets the office get caught up from all the activity that is generated from three days of meeting with clients.

Q. So how many hours a week do you think you are working, whether it is in the office or out of the office?
A. Right now with a staff member out on leave, I know it's much more than 60 hours and I don't quite honestly want to count them. But a year from now, I really think it would be much more back to those four good, solid work days. They are certainly 10 hour work days and then just a little bit over the weekend. So if I could get it to 50 hours when I am working, that would be terrific.

Q. What would you say your most successful marketing strategy has been?

A. Taking care of our clients. They know we are there for them and that has given us a rewarding relationship with clients. I tell our employees we are, "all in," meaning we are going to do everything we can to make it a good client experience, to make it as seamless as possible, and to let them know that they have a group of people that really care.

Q. So how tough were your first three years?

A. It was very difficult. I have had many people ask me if it was because I was a woman at a time when it was not very common to see a female broker in a Merrill-Lynch office. The percentages haven't increased that dramatically over the years. Lorraine and I have always joked that the one good thing about going to investor conferences all these years, we don't have to wait in line at the lady's room! But it was a difficult time. I think I would say the biggest one was just philosophical and I am not here to bash Merrill-Lynch, but just that environment was not a fit for my personality. When I went to my manager and said I am going to study for my CFP he said, "You should not spend your time on that; you should be calling more prospects." Needless to say I had a real problem with that. When I eventually found the independent financial planning space it was like, all the lights went on. I thought, "Oh, this is home for me. I get to build a business? I happen to be a financial planner, but I can build a good, solid, successful business and provide advice, but with my personality and with my goals." My first five years with Merrill-Lynch were difficult trying to figure out how I could do this in a way that I enjoyed and reflected my values.

Q. So what is your personal view of retirement for you?

A. For me it is to have this business exist beyond me. I tell the gang here and I mean it in all sincerity, I want to be dispensable. We have just poured ourselves into this business, but I want to retire at a young enough age where I can just really enjoy it. I am definitely not the type that's going to tell you that I am going to be here when I am 70. For me, it would be to ultimately have this business either taken over by employees or work with some type of arrangement where our values and philosophy carries on, which is very important to us. We definitely want each of our employees that are with us today, to work here for their entire career. That doesn't mean that I have to be here. That would be the ideal situation, along with a lot of travel and a lot of fun. I definitely enjoy working, but I can see beyond being a business owner and a financial planner. I definitely can see a time when I am 100% retired and I look forward to it, I love what I do but I look forward to that part of my life to.

Q. When do you see that happening?
A. I just turned 52. Lorraine will be 59 this summer. Ideally in the next five to seven years, I need to figure out what this next stage is going to be like. For me, I would like to, by age 60, be very much in the background.

Q. If you ever had the chance to meet Bernie Madoff, what would you tell him?
A. If he could safely be in a third world country, I would sentence him there to make whatever part of the world he was in better. He should be with people who struggle everyday to get by, to have him do some good and do that but in that type of environment where it is harsh, where it is difficult, where there are so many things that you and I get to take for granted or certainly be grateful for. That is where that man should be today.

Q. So if there was one thing you could change about the industry, what would it be?
A. I would say – back to our earlier discussion – is not being defensive about being paid. I would want our value to be realized. It is a tremendous ability to be able to take all of the knowledge and expertise that we have, and be able to

provide value to people – so don't be defensive about it, and don't minimize it, and don't make it a commodity. If clients say, "Well you are at 1.5%. I can get it at ¾%." Don't even engage in that type of an argument and understand your value.

Q. Any last comments to potential clients or people coming into the industry that you would want to share?

A. I would say to clients that it's more important than ever to work with somebody that you trust and that you understand. Discipline is going to be a very important part of it because none of us have that crystal ball, but I do think we all, as investors, have tremendous opportunity for the long term. It may look like we are making a mistake in the short run because something goes against us, but we have to be able to see the forest through the trees, to see the long-term view. I think it's a great time to be an investor, but you need to align yourself with someone you trust, and stay focused. For someone just looking to get into the business, I would say it is an incredible career choice. It gives you an amazing amount of flexibility. You get to use many skills. You get to make a difference in people's lives, which is so important and fulfilling.

"Retirement at 65 is ridiculous. When I was 65, I still had pimples."

-George Burns

"You spend 30 years with people and you can really make a difference in their lives. It's a big deal and I get a lot of psychic reward from that."
Dave Petso, Petso Financial Consultants, LLC

Dave Petso has been in the financial planning business for about 30 years. He moved to Boise, Idaho after high school with the idea that he would be going to school at night. He brought his girlfriend, now wife, along for the experience. At the time, the critics of the plan outweighed the supporters. However, it's all worked out fairly well looking back over those 30 some years. Dave needed work and it was suggested he get an insurance license and sell insurance. So at 18 years old, he got his insurance license, turned 19, and then 18 months later got his securities license. He then left the insurance company and went on from there.

Dave currently has his CFP. He has three independent reps and five employees with approximately $470M assets under management. Dave's company specializes in income and retirement planning along with endowments.

Q. Was a career in financial planning a childhood ambition?
A. No, but, actually somewhat. Shortly after the true recognition that I was not tall enough, quick enough, and couldn't jump, professional basketball seemed a bit of a stretch. Then I really was quite fascinated with the markets and things like that, so I actually started buying stocks and thought I wanted to be stock broker. So it's related somewhat. I was probably around 12 when I opened a casino in my basement and realized I had a knack for numbers and that I enjoyed it.

Q. What is your greatest motivation for being a planner?

A. Well, it's changed. Obviously, when you can't pay bills, money is a very good motivator. Today, the reason I stay in the business and work as hard as I do now isn't financial, that's the score keeping part of it, but now it is because I absolutely love the business. I am intuitive with people; I know how to get to the root problems that maybe they don't know. You spend 30 years with people and you can really make a difference in their lives. It's a big deal and I get a lot of psychic reward from that.

Q. What do you see as being the greatest challenge in meeting client needs?

A. Its two things. Obviously, there's time constraints in meeting client's needs, so time to effectively do it, that also plays into the business structure that we have been working very hard at changing, and we are getting there. We are structuring and I now have a team. We are a full-time team of three licensed CFP's that are solely working with my clients. Secondly, there's just no question that human emotions play against us. We are cavemen and we think analytically. That works fine for tracking the food – you follow the tracks and at the end of it, hopefully there's some game you can kill. We still have the same brain. When everything is really good and rosy and the outlook is great, we move with the news. Take the Beijing Olympics. If we wanted something very current – then we've got to invest in China because we just hear so many good stories about it and they are going to dominate the world in 25 years. And shortly afterwards the market falls 60%, all people do is talk about the market being off 60%. But the underlying Chinese story has done nothing more than get better. They continue to make more money and their growth is still great, but now with 60% off, everybody can only talk about the problems. Why in the world would I invest in China?

So dealing with people's caveman brain – that we all have – is the difficult part, dealing with calming people down, tempering euphoria. The pain of the loss is much more severe than the gain. I don't need to tell you that, but that is really the biggest trick, to get people thinking counter-intuitively.

Q. When addressing a new client in the early stages of their career, what's the single most important piece of advice you give them?
A. Start something. I learned this when I was first starting out. I got my first big break in '84 working with the school district. I don't know why they said "yes" to such a young pup. I was about 22 or 23-years old. They said I could go in and talk to all the teachers there over the summer and it brought me from that barely scraping by level, to now being able to make a living. Not a big living, but a living. So being a salesperson you don't want to leave without getting something. It really taught me a valuable lesson which is that you can start them off at $25 a month, and then come back next year when they get a little raise and then go to $35, and then to $50, and then to $75, and then $100. If they waited until they could do $250 a month, something "significant," then you never start. So to summarize, I don't care what you think you can or can't afford, just start something. It's the principle; just start. Secondly, would be to stay out of debt. Third, I would tell them that if you work hard and most of the world does not, then you will be easily recognized.

Q. What is the greatest challenge facing this industry?
A. Finding the next generation. They are not rainmakers. I liken this more to the baby-boom generation. We are all risk takers. As kids we would disappear in the morning and come home by dark. We weren't to be seen in the house all summer long and if that meant you burned down the field, well, that was a natural occurrence. If it meant you're building jumps and daring each other to jump over the barbed wire fence on your bike, go down to the river to swim, that's what you did. That stayed with us. Now we send our kids out in rubber suits to go out and roller blade. It's just a different

world, and I am not saying they are wrong, but this generation is unwilling to do what we did to be successful, to work 14 hours a day, if that's what it took, and have ten people tell you every day to piss off. They won't do it.

Q. What frustrates you about the industry?
A. Probably the ethics, the "quick buck" ethics. As far as governing bodies steering us, I have never seen a governing body do anything for me. It's always doing something to me, so I have a difficult time thinking that there is an organization that could really do that. If there was, it would probably be something like the SEC going back to their real roots, which is supposed to be to make the playing field more favorable to the small investor. Period.

Q. What would you tell a college graduate with a degree in finance, considering your chosen career?
A. I have a lot of people call and ask for advice getting into this business, and I typically tell them that it's extremely difficult to get started, and you will make no money for awhile if you are doing it at all right. That being said, it is extremely rewarding if you hang in there. Of course, we all know the numbers that very few survive the first three to five years. Above all that, they really do have to have a passion in two areas, and that is that they have to be passionate about people and they have to enjoy this business. This business changes so fast and it is extremely hard to keep up on things. You better like what you are doing. You better love what you are doing.

Q. Do you feel the industry today is overly complicated and the products too few or too many?
A. Of course, particularly if you want to pick on annuities or REITS or packaged products. At the same time though, that's not always an easy answer to give because there are some new products I would love to see. So I am asking for more even as I am asking for less, I am a perfect politician on this one. What I would like to see, which I think is going to be

coming, is going to be more income products designed for retirees.

Q. Look at the last three years dealing with three different client types. The first would be somebody who is a new investor in their early 20's, then someone who is an established investor in their mid 40's, and then somebody who is on the verge of retiring, how significant is our current economy, either from an opportunistic standpoint or the detriment to that individual?

A. I guess from their perspective they are all scared to death with the added uncertainty of jobs, pensions, and health care. However, it's terribly troubling for retirees who have grown up in an America they thought they understood. They are scared to death of the socialism that the current congress and administration are pushing. They are scared to death of the deficits; they don't understand how they can ever be paid and what that means for the dollars they have. It's just a completely different world, and within that world for 10 or 12 years now, the market has gone nowhere. So the things they relied on and grew up with and built their wealth with, have done nothing positive. They think I'm a Pollyanna when I tell them that I think it will be okay. So those folks are the ones that are really struggling most.

The established investor who is in a stable job is in a much more comfortable position, but still doesn't like the world they are looking at. If you are in an accumulation phase, this is the best stuff that can happen for you. The analogy that I give people is if you are going to build a dam and you didn't have all the gravel for that dam right now, you have a 20 timeline. Would you like the price of gravel to go up as you are accumulating it, or would you like it to stay stable or maybe even decline in price so you are not paying more for it? Of course, that's an analogy to buying shares. If they are particularly risk adverse, it's also opportunistic to use some kind of equity income fund that has regular dividends that they can see go back in. It also helps give them a more stable flow going forward. This is a phenomenal opportunity for people to be thinking of the next 10 to 20 years, not the past 10.

Q. So do you operate a particular portfolio strategy? Active managers? Do you use third-party people?

A. We use both, but it depends on the size of the client's account. We are still willing to take the guy who comes in making less than $250K. He may hear me on the radio about getting something started; it's difficult to turn people away. At $250K and above, we manage it. We are relatively active.

Q. Have you become more active or less active over these last three years?

A. We pretend to be more active. I hire active management within the portfolios. I hire eclectic managers, in other words we put them in the portfolios. We, during the meltdown, found that people were terrified and really needed us to do something. When they called, we gave them a feeling of empowerment, and I don't like the word because it's an Oprah word, but people need to be empowered. Just by making minor changes we were able to get them to hang in there during a time when they just couldn't sell, but they couldn't stay. With just making minor changes, we got them to feel like they had done something and could hang tough. But we are less active and I have a list of 10 investment commandments that are really for me, one of those is to not overtrade because we all have a tendency to overtrade. But I also don't believe you can buy and hold forever. Companies change, circumstances change, but chasing after what worked yesterday is a sure way to make sure it stops working.

Q. Is the greater challenge running the company or managing clients?

A. Good question. The business has become more of a challenge – clients are fun and I will just say it: I am good at it. I am good with clients, so that part is easy. It is always a challenge when the market goes down a thousand points, but it's much more challenging now that we have grown, so it's a good problem. Now that we have grown to a size where the business is consuming a lot of my thoughts and how we can get it better structured, the greatest challenge is the business.

Q. What does your average work week look like?
A. Monday mornings I get up and I watch TV, just a quick three minute thing breaking down the coming week or something like that. Then I hit the office, which is about 7:30am and I am here sometimes until 5 or 6:00pm. In the summer I like to go out and play golf. I don't read a lot of my stuff during the day because I don't have time. I read the paper at night, but I like the industry so it's no big deal.

Q. What do you consider your single most successful marketing strategy?
A. Well, that would have to be the radio which led to TV and everything else. They feed off of each other, but radio still has greater value because it's more time, and although people can see me on TV, they can really get to know me on the radio. Radio probably has a bigger impact, but there is a bigger TV audience. When you combine the two, it is pretty powerful from a "getting to know me" perspective. I don't have an initial "get to know me" meeting because they already know me.

Q. How tough were the first three years as a planner?
A. Let me just say that I would not want to go do that again.

Q. What is your personal view of retirement?
A. I think my dad has it about right. I can't imagine not continuing to do this, but I am not going to do it at this pace. I would like to be involved until I lose my brains or am dead. Maybe I'll lose my brains and not know it. I enjoy the interaction

with people and I enjoy feeling like I matter in their lives. Right now, I can't imagine not doing it.

Q. What is your expectation of your firm for when you retire?
A. You know, I've got to say that's one of the things about CPG. One of the reasons I joined is that it is time to figure that out, isn't it? I could kick over anytime and like anybody who is any good at this business, there are hundreds of people I really care about that we service and I want them to continue with us. I don't trust anybody else out there to do it.

Q. If you had the opportunity to talk to Bernie Madoff, what would you say?
A. Why would you do that? I have found, and certainly with somebody with as much experience as him, he was already successful, that money chases you. It chases you once you lay the foundation and he already had that. I just don't understand. I really don't.

Q. If there was one thing in the industry that you could change, what would it be?
A. I guess I would lower and flatten compensation on product sales.

Q. Any last comments before I let you go?
A. I guess my only comment is this is the greatest industry in the world for people who don't have any other special talents. You can learn and grow. You've just got to be a hard worker and give a rip about people. You have to have that commitment and that sensitivity to the human kind.

18

"Financial advisor means, just like any professional, we have to really seize the opportunity to figure out what the issues are for the client."
Jeff Rattiner, JR Financial Group, Inc.

Jeff Rattiner is CPA, a CFP, and an educator. He has a tax practice in Scottsdale and Denver as well as a financial planning practice. But today Jeff is primarily involved in his training practice. Conservatively speaking in recent years Jeff has participated in the training of several thousand CFP's. Jeff started out at Arthur-Andersen as an auditor, back in the early 1980's in New York. He is a self confessed creative individual and confesses "you can't be a creative auditor unless you want to end up in jail," so quickly changed directions. He has been the director of professional development and corporate sponsorship for the Institute of Certified Financial Planners (ICFP), and was employed as the director of technical standards for the Certified Financial Planner Board of Standards (CFP Board). He developed practice standards and reference guides for CFP licensees to use in the practice of personal financial planning, as well was employed as technical manager in the personal financial planning (PFP) division of the American Institute of Certified Public Accountants (AICPA) in New York City. He has eight books published on various subjects related to planning.

Q. What is your general view of the financial planning industry today? Is it in good order? Is it serving itself well? Are we under too much scrutiny?
A. Well, I can tell you from an educator standpoint that the people that are actually doing planning are not as educated as they should be. I can tell you from all these people that come into my classes that it's amazing the types of questions I get. They are good people, they are honest, decent people, but if

I had a million dollars in an IRA and was relying on someone here that really didn't know basic stuff about IRA rollovers and so forth, I would be kind of nervous. I don't think a lot of that shows to the client though. So from that perspective, I think there are a lot of people in here that are not operating at full capacity from an education standpoint.

I think what they need to learn, instead of learning to sell product, is to sell processes so people understand what the issues are. Then the beauty of that is they are going to go through the whole rig-and-roll of what the client needs and uncover a lot more needs. They'll end up making more money and doing a better job for the client because they have addressed everything upfront. Instead, they take a very tactical approach where they are going in there and try to sell a particular project. Uncover the need and what will happen is you are going to do a better job with the client because you are going to get them more in tune with what they really need.

Q. Now, with that said, do you think that the educational short fall is true academic education or is it purely experiential. Are students coming into the classes too early and do they need to be mentored for a period of time?

A. It's a combination. The academic level is going to help people understand the key concepts, the practical level which we emphasize in our program is "how to do it." So you need both halves. The CFP board tests on both the academic and the practical. If somebody has been practicing a lot longer, that will help them on the actual exam, but there's still a bunch of academic stuff that they need to know. The problem is that when people come into this industry, they are

> "The reason why the CFP's are second-class citizens to a lot of people is because they have come from an insurance and an investment orientation as a salesperson."

taught how to sell. They are not taught how to think like a professional. They are not taught to think like a CPA or an attorney. You go to somebody, you pay X-dollars an hour, you expect them to come up with very clever solutions, uncover the real issues, and stuff like that. There's not enough training in this industry. I have trained over the years a lot of big banks, some insurance companies, and a lot of different schools around the country. The people in there are smart people, but they don't know how to think through the big picture. They are not strategic in their orientation and that's a huge shortfall. So people are coming in to cover a specific need and thereby selling product only.

My thinking is that within 10 years, a lot of the distribution channels that we see today are going to go away. You can go through the Internet and do everything you need to relatively inexpensively. I will give you a great example: Travel agents. When we used to travel that was the first thing we would do, is go to the travel agent. You don't do that now. You go to Expedia.com, you might contact United directly. Today you can buy insurance and annuities and other stuff like that too because there's really not that much of a difference in the overall product. If people understand how to look at the big picture, then the individual components don't really mean as much and that means everybody has similar products out there. Nobody is shattering the other. So people have to really learn how to think and what their true value is in assessing the need, coming up with what the real exposures are for the client, and then coming up with a solution or recommendation. I am saying a lot of them are short-sighted because none of them were taught how to do that.

Q. That is a theme that comes up often, how do you simplify the difference between product and process?
A. I can tell you first hand because I am responsible for process. I have worked for companies where we have talked about

product, but it's like I tell my students: I am driving from Los Angeles to New York. I know I have to go east and I know I have to go north, but I if I don't have a road map it is going to take me lot more time to get to where I need to go, and the shortest distance between two points is a straight line and if I can figure out how to stay on course, which is what financial planning is all about, then I am going to be in a lot better shape. Some people that are real sales people say, "I can bypass all that," and I tell these guys, just like I tell the CPA's out there, the Internet is changing the way we do business and if you don't jump on the planning band wagon – you are going to be lost.

I will give you another great analogy I use: 100 years ago the railroads were the most dominant form of transportation. They basically transported people and goods all over the place. They were kind of arrogant about it at the same time, but over the course of years, not too many years thereafter, you had automobiles, you had airplanes, and you had other modes of transportation. The railroads made a very poor calculation by not realizing they were in the transportation business, not the railroad business. The deal is we are financial advisors. Financial advisor means, just like any professional, we have to really seize the opportunity to figure out what the issues are for the client. Once we do that, we will be in a much better position to come up with a solution so the client can do all the things that they earmarked for themselves over their lifetime in a very succinct and strong manner. If they are able to do that and we are able to teach people that, then we will elevate ourselves to be on the same level as attorneys, CPA's, and other professionals.

Q. Why is it that planners, even CFP's, feel themselves to be second-class citizens compared to their professional peer groups, CPA's and lawyers.

A. I would say there's some truth in that as voiced through consumers and even felt by a small number of CFP certificants.

Now again, I have a very unique advantage because I teach a lot of CPA's around the country and they are head and shoulders above the CFP's in terms of certain types of technical knowledge they possess. This is because they were required to take more technical types of courses as part of their college curriculum and adhere to heavy CE requirements thereafter. But I tell the CFP audience that I teach, I say, "It's not a big deal. Remember: CPA's have a 75-year head start over us. We will eventually get there, just like how lawyers had a 100+ year start before CPA's." So I think the thing to remember is that we are not second-class citizens, we are just in a younger profession. I know many high-level, very bright CFP's and they can stand with anyone. I think it really depends on the training. I think if a young guy is coming out of school and he is sent to an insurance company or a brokerage company, with just learning how to sell, he's never going to get to that level. If they say to him, "You know what? We have some time. Take six months, get your CFP, get all the type of relevant training so you can come in and think outside the box," those people tend to be a lot more successful. The reason why the CFP's are second-class citizens to a lot of people is because they have come from an insurance and an investment orientation as a salesperson. Their emphasis is on how to sell that particular type of product line.

Q. Are there global changes you think the industry could impose upon itself that would make it a better place for its participants and the clients?
A. Absolutely. Think of it from this perspective: if you want to be a CPA, in a lot of states you have to get 124 hours or 150 hours of college. We have a college requirement, but we don't have any real coursework designed to make sure we get there other than six classes of financial planning. Perhaps it should be taken to the college level and basically work it in, just like any other major. Some schools are doing that, but not enough. This way when they come out, they will really have a true understanding with how to help people.

Q. Currently the points of entry into this industry are all examination based. Are these examinations relevant for the majority of financial planning clients?

A. I always tease my classes about the Series 7, and the Series 6, and the Series 66, etc. I make fun of those exams because they are very easy compared to the CFP, number one. Number two people say, "Oh, I have passed the Series 7; so how much more difficult can the CFP exam be?" And I tell them that investment planning, as a whole, is just 19% of the CFP exam. The Series 7 portion of that might be less than half of that, so it's really not representative. So even though you may have a Series 7, you are not well versed in talking with clients about retirement issues, insurance issues, and income tax issues, the estate issues, and so forth. So you really need to learn the big picture. Do you want to be a trader? Do you want to be a stockbroker? Then you don't need anything greater than a Series 7. I tell people that's not enough and if we don't add value then your job will be assumed by the Internet. "I don't care how good you are; you can't compete against free. You just can't." If somebody knows they can go and buy an insurance product on the Internet and can get it to 50 to 60% of what the true cost is, don't you think people are going to go in that direction?

Q. Would you like to see an educational minimum, such as a CFP, invoked?

A. Think about it: If you want to be a professional, how can you call yourself a professional if you sit for one day and you study for an exam and then that's suppose to make you a professional? You have no training. Can you imagine your doctor operating on you? "Here, let me take a week of med school here and we will get this going." Or, "We'll just focus on the foot and that's all you need to know. You don't need to know about all the other aspects of the body?" That's ludicrous. So you have to come in there and you have to say, "If I understand how the whole picture works, it will be easier for me to diagnose what the issues are and come up with appropriate solutions. Number one, it will do a better job for the client, and number two it's going to make me a lot more money. If they use that approach, these guys are going to do really well.

Q. What challenges specifically do you see facing these guys and gals?

A. Some of the younger advisors out there don't have enough grey hair. What that means is they don't have enough real world experience. If I am a 60 year old guy and I have $5 million dollars in the bank and some 25 year old kid comes up to me and tells me what I should be doing with my money, I am going to be a little suspect. That's the reality of it. I think that is the biggest challenge that these younger guys have to overcome.

Q. In your experience, how have people addressed and succeeded in that environment? What do they need to do other than dye their hair?

A. Well, they need to be well versed in the area. If they are CFP's or they have some type of professional designation, they can go in there and show them with charts and graphs and story lines and experiences. Even just reading books to get examples on incorporating information from clients into real world experience will help them. But they are not going to be trained appropriately if they are just sitting for some nonsense insurance exam or investment exam. If you really want to be a professional, an advisor, then you need to be educated and that education encompasses financial planning, which is a process, not a product, and it helps to look at the big picture. If you understand the big picture strategically, then you can fill in the tactical stuff pretty easily.

"The primary reason so few Americans achieve financial independence is the lack of self-discipline."

-Tom Peters

"I find that most of the time people are worried about their compensation first and the client second. I would try to figure out how to reverse those two."
Jim Regitz, Newport Advisory, LLC

Jim Regitz has been a financial planner for 26 years. Once Jim finished college, he went to work for Signa Financial Advisors, which today is called Sagemart Consulting. He stayed with them for 11years. Jim started as a planner but ended up in sales management, ultimately running their Los Angeles office. In 1995 he left the insurance company, BD World, and took the leap to independence. Jim's firm manages approx $500M directly, and via their branch registered representatives.

Q. Was a career in financial planning something you considered through the earlier stages of your school career?
A. I am not sure what I wanted to do back then. My dad has always been very much a financial guy; he has always been running his budgets and worried about his investments. So I grew up watching that and it was something that always very much interested me. I kind of knew I would end up in the business aspect, most likely the finance and sales side of things. I guess I spent the latter part of high school knowing where I would end up.

Q. What is your greatest motivation today for staying in the business?
A. Being cutting edge, that's very simple. One of the things I learned is the speed at which this industry changes and the technical changes, tax laws and other things. The thing that motivates me most is the next thing that I need to be able to bring to my clients, be that new technical idea or new concepts. The new investment world seems to be more feeding

at break neck speed, and trying to stay on the cutting edge of that is what gets my juices flowing.

Q. What would you consider to be the greatest challenge in meeting a client's needs?

A. As our business has gotten to be more complicated, the products are changing, the concepts are changing, and tax laws are changing. The problem is that there are generally so many complications in a client's situation, that the difficulty is being able to break that down into a simple enough way to explain it to a client. Explain it in a way they can understand enough to take action on them, but at the same time not so totally overwhelm them with technical things that they then are frozen and don't make decisions. I have found that a bit difficult the last couple years.

> "So the hours tend to be long, but I never miss a family event, I never miss a baseball game. Those things are important to me."

Q. When you are addressing somebody younger who maybe looking for guidance on their future, what is the single most important piece of advice that you would give them?

A. Probably the first thing I would say, particularly for younger people, is don't do things you don't understand. Take some time initially to understand what you are doing, and what the recommendations are. Spend some time educating yourself on the basics because you need to be asking good questions when you meet with an advisor so you don't get taken advantage of in the end.

Q. What would you consider today to be the greatest challenge facing the industry as a whole?

A. The next generation. When I came into the industry, there were more structured ways to get into this business and get trained in various aspects. A lot of those have gone away.

The insurance companies are not really at the level that they were 10, 15, 20 years ago. The wire houses are different; there aren't a lot of really good ways for young people to get into the industry. We are creating a very big problem for ourselves because there is not a clear career path for a lot of these kids coming out of Texas Tech and various other places around the country where they are developing financial planning degrees. We just aren't developing great places for those younger people to come in, and I think as an industry we are missing the boat substantially.

Q. What do you find frustrates you the most in the industry?
A. I think there are two. I tell client's the same thing every time. I think one of the two biggest frustrations I have in the industry are incompetence and ethics. It's because there is so much money in our industry; you get a lot of people out there that run around making recommendations to clients that they don't really understand. They do it because of the financial incentives to do it and if they truly understood what was going on, the recommendations would be different. That bothers me very much; I put that into an incompetence level and then from there you also have people who are intelligent and kind of do get it. Yet they choose to sell particular products or things inadequately, and that gets into the ethics issue. I think our industry has a great deal of both confidence and lack of ethics in a lot of situations. Ignorance in some and lack of ethics in others – that would be my major frustrations.

Q. Is it safe to say that you have obviously enjoyed your career and you wouldn't look back with regret and wish you had done something differently?
A. No, absolutely not. I have some pretty strong religious convictions and I feel very much that I have been led down a path and been strained in a particular way. Although I have been in the industry 26 years, I am only 48 years old. So that's actually a very exciting thing because I know the next 20 years

will be a lot of fun for us as I have been able to put a lot of experience, and been able to build some infrastructure. The next stage should be a lot more fun.

Q. Let's say a college graduate out of Texas Tech presents himself to you in your office and is looking for some guidance. What would you tell him?

A. Take your time in looking for the right mix. Know what you are looking to do with your career and then be sure to find the right firm to do that. We were kind of talking earlier about how the industry tends to hire people like that and either shove them into an administrative role, or shove them into a sales role. I think it is important for a person coming out of school to understand what it is they like about the industry and what it is that they would like to do in the long run. Again, if the person is very analytical and very good at building and developing financial plans, that person probably shouldn't get stuck into an administrative role or shouldn't get stuck in a sales role. They should be able to find a position where they can make a lucrative career doing the things they are good at. That's not necessarily jumping at the first job that is out there just to gain a little experience, but look for the right firm. They are out there; it's a matter of finding the right mix and the right firm that is going to be able to evolve that desired position.

Q. Do you feel the industry today is overly complicated by virtue of just general structure, but also the products that we have to contend with?

A. Yes but more importantly, I think it's overly confusing. If I am a client, the way the regulations have been set up in the hope of disclosure has made it absolutely confusing to me to understand in any way, shape, or form, what I am dealing with. There are fees versus commissions, RIA's versus independent BD's, FCC versus Finra, etc. You go through all the way people are positioned and the result is the end client doesn't really get it, they simply don't understand. There is no legal requirement to call yourself a financial planner. You can call yourself whatever you want and it makes it very confusing for a consumer to understand what they are getting. So I think the way we are setup as an industry is confusing to the end client. I don't think the products really confuse it, but I think it's how we are regulated and how we hold ourselves out to the public that creates the problems.

Q. If you've got a new investor who is young and at the early stage of their career, an established investor, and a retiree – how significant is our current economy versus the prior 20-25 years?

A. The current economy is particularly important. I would probably take that order and reverse it in terms of how important it is. Obviously for a retiree, the current economic environment as it relates to performances or portfolios is huge. Generally somebody at the retirement level obviously can't afford a substantial downside risk in their portfolio. So that becomes more important. For a younger person who is invested for the longer term, the economy becomes a little less important, although I don't know if I would tie it as much to an age issue as I would to an individual's risk parameters. I think as an industry and as a country, most people end up investing in stuff that they don't quite get. There may be a 65 year old person that has a fairly high risk tolerance and then again there might be a 25 year old person who has no risk at all. So I would probably answer that more in a way that people need to understand what their downsides are as they start to invest. We as an industry need to explain that better to our clients. Portfolio construction needs to be matched up with the risk that somebody is willing to accept. I am not sure that we do a great job of that as an industry. In 2008, if

"Spend some time educating yourself on the basics because you need to be asking good questions when you meet with an advisor so you don't get taken advantage of in the end."

you looked at people who were largely invested in the US and large cap international stocks, and those people lost 40-50%, most people would probably have said, "I am not willing to accept that risk," yet statistically, if you look at it, it was certainly a possibility that you could lose that much money. As an industry, we generally lay that out to a client for them to understand there is a possibility you can lose that kind of money. Most people wouldn't take the risk if they truly understood it.

Q. Within your investment portfolios, do you run a traditional modern portfolio theory allocation or are you more actively managing accounts? Do you use third party money managers?

A. What I didn't talk about in my background when I left Signa back in 1995, was one of the reasons why I left. I felt that the investment side of our work was a little weaker and I had an opportunity to affiliate with some guys who had a relationship with Cullen Associates in San Francisco, which is a very large institutional investment management consulting firm. So I was able to get trained in that world and started building our own asset allocation models and doing our own manager selections. I was very involved in modern portfolio theory from that point forward. We built our portfolios until probably early 2000. When that market started to fall apart, we started asking different questions about modern portfolio theory and how it applies. We started to realize that the theory was great, but I don't think Harry Markowitz ever intended for it to be applied the way that we as an industry were applying it. So we started to re-look at that and started to change some things. Ultimately, we ended up adding some different asset classes that were not correlated and alternative investments. We started looking at some different things that were more tactical in their approach and that just escalated quite a bit here in the last 20-24 months or so. So we do not apply straight modern portfolio theory, we do something that's got its roots in modern portfolio theory but its application and implementation is a bit more tactical.

Q. You mentioned 24 months – was that change coincidental to the market and what's gone on the last two to three years?
A. When the change happened for us it was probably 2006-2007; we wanted to start to understand hedge funds. The hedge fund world was starting to become very popular and we weren't sure we even wanted to offer them. What we started to realize was that the data that we were getting from various asset allocation software and various research things, were packaging data in ways that we weren't comfortable with. We were coming up with different conclusions and different answers. So we stopped using a lot of the pre-packaged modern portfolio theory stuff particularly with the date ranges they were using. I don't want to say it was in anticipation of the crash, I would say that our need to understand what was going on in hedge funds and private equity drove our decisions to look at things a little differently. I think that ended up resulting in us approaching our allocations differently, and then obviously the world kind of fell apart there.

Q. So what does your average work week look like?
A. My work week is not a short one. I work about 50-60 hours; probably 50 on average, but it's flexible and I think that's the key. There are days that I may work 12 or 15 hours and then the next day I am out of here at 3pm so I can go home and coach my son's T-ball team. So the hours tend to be long, but I never miss a family event, I never miss a baseball game. Those things are important to me. The work tends to be hard, but not at the cost of family.

Q. As a firm, what would you consider to be the most successful marketing strategy that you have deployed?
A. Absolutely client referrals. When you spend time building a practice – like I had to do at 21 – which is really difficult, and you build relationships with clients, those relationships are

absolutely just golden to you. That is what you have spent your life building. Our best marketing is really just serving our clients because by serving our clients, you end up getting a fair amount of referrals to other people because they can see how they do. The absolute best way I can build us from a marketing level, is by spending more time and doing more things for our existing clientele.

Q. How tough were those first three years for you when you left college?
A. Oh they were horrible! The way that we built it, our business, was dealing with business owners. We were kind of dealing more in a business to business environment. We were back in 1984 so the environment was a little different, but we were cold calling. I would spend about 20-25% of my time just calling business owners in an attempt to set up an additional meeting with them in their place of business. That's what we did. I spent pretty much one full day a week and part of another day just cold calling and setting up appointments. So for three years that's what I did until the referral base developed adequately to allow the business to go forward. The one thing about it that I really appreciate was I didn't start this business by going and hitting up friends and family and all the people that I knew. I worked generally with people I didn't know. I really don't go after the people I know in my social environment. Most of our clients are people who have been referred to us. It never felt good to me back then, and it still doesn't feel good to me now, to go to people I know.

Q. What is your personal view of retirement for yourself?
A. I can't imagine that I will ever retire. I see myself eventually working with some key clients only and be the vision person, and work on strategic planning. I think part of it will have to do with my kids as well. I have pretty young kids and if they were ever to show some interest in the business, that would probably change my opinion a little bit too. I would probably try to be more actively involved and hope that they would

want to come in at some point, but they are still way too young to know that. So that would have some bearing on it.

Q. If you made the assumption that your kids did not have an interest, would you look to succeed it internally or would you look to monetize it quickly and sell it to some third party?
A. I think it's really hard to answer until you are there. If there are people in the firm and I have done my job as a business owner, I should have raised up people to allow it to continue if I am not here. It would occur naturally and that would be ideal. If I don't do it successfully and I get to a spot where I am now 65 and my kids are not coming into the business and I haven't done a great job of building out the next generation, then I really have no choice but to monetize and sell it out on the outside. We've got about 40 advisors under our branch and I see a number of them at different positions. One of the problems I find with a lot of them is they are getting to that point where they are now considering retiring or within a few years of retiring and they really just don't have a succession plan in place. There isn't anybody to step in. Their only option at that point is to sell it. Because you become so close to your clients and you spend so much time with them, there are not many people in the industry that are comfortable saying, "I want to sell it to the highest bidder and walk away." Most of the time people want to allow that practice to continue, but they just haven't built out an infrastructure to allow that to happen. So they are really stuck.

Q. You actually raised a good point earlier that Madoff himself was a fee-based planner. If you had the chance to sit down and talk to him, what would you talk about?
A. That's kind of interesting. Rarely do I find that people set out to be unethical and take advantage of people and steal money. I am guessing he didn't set out to do that in the beginning. There was an inflection point somewhere along the way, something happened, a bad quarter, something somewhere got him to deviate off his original plan. If I had

a chance to talk with him in an open and honest and way, I would like to understand what that point was because I think that's where the take away from this whole thing is. I think everyone of us in business, in our industry, have those lessons to be learned. I suspect there is that one little thing that didn't seem like it was a big deal and it became one small change, which became two small changes, which became three and before you know it you got behind the 8-ball and couldn't get out of it. So I think I would love to be able to understand how he got to that spot because he obviously didn't just start there.

Q. If there was one thing in this industry that you could change, what would it be?

A. Let me answer it with an illustration. When I first got into the industry the thing that attracted me to Signa was that I worked with a guy named Stuart Smith. He was an advisor for a lot of years and he built his whole practice, and ultimately trained a number of advisors, on a "serve first" philosophy. The philosophy was to put the client first and the compensation side will take care of itself on the backside. If I could change one thing in the industry, it would be to not just use the words of service and ethics, but to really get people to a spot where they are doing what is really just in the best interest of their clients, and let the compensation take care of itself. I just find that most of the time people are worried about their compensation first and the client becomes second. I would probably try to figure out how to reverse those two.

"If they are willing to take the time and learn the craft, it's a wonderful industry to work in."
Jared Roskelley, Jackson Financial Advisors

Jared Roskelley has been in the financial planning business about 13 years. He worked his way through college in the industry whilst studying finance. Jared is a partner in the firm working alongside Bob Jackson, the founder of their company and president. The firm operates as an OSJ for six senior advisors that all maintain their own books and business. However the working relationships within the group are extremely collaborative, the independent reps being more an internal component than an external one. They manage about $140 million in both commission and fee products, and they consider themselves to be a boutique firm with a focus on retirement planning for families and small business owners. The boutique moniker comes from the collaborative nature and strengths that they bring from their other advisors to the table.

Q. Was it a career aspiration of yours early in life to follow this path?
A. I grew up in the business. My dad was one of the first Certified Financial Planners (CFP's), so I grew up with an exposure to it. I can honestly say that it wasn't something I aspired to; not because I didn't like the business, but because I didn't have enough of an understanding of the business. I knew my dad went to work every day and he helped people with investments, taxes and retirement planning, but so much of that was foreign to me. While in college I discovered that I had a propensity for accounting and finance. About two years into my degree program was when I actually came back into the business and started with my dad as a paraplanner. It was then I got more exposure to how we were

helping people. That's when the passion started to develop for being a financial planner.

Q. So what is your greatest motivation today for being in the business?
A. I love working with clients and being able to make a meaningful difference in their lives.

Q. What do you think the greatest challenge in meeting client needs is today?
A. I think the greatest challenge is aligning the expectations of the client with solutions that make sense. Our observation of our clients is that they all have a high tolerance for risk, they are just loss adverse. That can be a difficult expectation to manage.

Q. So you've got somebody who walks into your office that's just exiting college, they have a good career path ahead of them. What's the single most important piece of advice that you would give them?
A. Probably the single most important piece of advice would be to start thinking about their future early, and understand how the decisions that they make at 21, 22, and 23, are going to have consequences, not just when they are 30, 40, and 50+.

Q. What do you consider to be the greatest challenge facing the industry?
A. I would say trust. The more the news is full of the Bernie Madoffs and the Goldman Sachs, the less likely consumers are to look to us to being a trusted advisor and a voice of reason.

Q. What frustrates you the most about the industry?
A. That there isn't a minimum practice standard for advisors. There are multi-level marketing firms out there that recruit people with no experience or any financial background. They

then train them to go and sell a product. Who knows if the solution is a good fit for the client? All that matters is that a sale is made so that the rep can move on to the next.

I just wish that advisors would have to adhere to a minimum practice standard. Then consumers could have some confidence that our industry provides well researched, fiduciary-type advice. Until we get those standards in place, it's going to be difficult to overcome the challenge of trust.

Q. If you had the chance to follow a different career, would you?
A. If I wasn't color blind I would have loved to have been an Air Force pilot! But seriously, I couldn't see any other career that would have provided me with as much challenge and satisfaction. I didn't understand what I was getting into when I started, but I am very grateful for how it has turned out.

Q. If a graduate stood in your office with a degree in finance and was considering a similar career path to your own, what advice would you give them?
A. The best advice, I think, would be to get yourself as much exposure to as many areas of this business as you can because you are going to need it. That first five years is critical. The more you understand how the various aspects of taxes, estate planning, investments and even compliance/trading integrate, the more productive you are going to be in your career and the more successful you are going to be in helping others.

Q. Do you feel the industry today is overly complicated in the products that have to be dealt with? Are they too few, too many?
A. I think it could be simplified, yes. Right now, the current structure is difficult to understand. All of the regulation is intended to protect the consumer, but it is so thick that it

is difficult for consumers to understand how they are protected.

Q. You have three clients: one is a new investor, one is in their mid-40's and has a bit of a portfolio and is established in their career, and you've got a retiree. How significant is this current economy to them as individuals?

A. I think we have all seen those charts that have come out where if you had a person retire in 1980 versus a person retiring in 1990 with the same amount of money, how different their retirement aspirations would turn out. The next decade is going to be tough.

Retirees are going to expect more from their savings. Many retiree-aged people are entering retirement underfunded. They are hoping to keep working in retirement and that their kids will be able to support them.

There is going to be a big need for a paradigm shift. Retirement used to be seen as a rite of passage, but based on where we are now, it is going to be for those who prepare early and maintain a disciplined approach.

Q. If you look at your typical client portfolio, would you consider it to be inspired by modern portfolio theory? Do you actively manage? Do you use third-party money managers?

A. Yes, to all three. For years and years we subscribed to modern portfolio theory and as long as the markets went up, it worked great. What we discovered, though, is that modern portfolio theory has two fatal assumptions: one is that it assumes all investors react rationally given all information at all times; the other major fault is that it takes into account a subject test group

> *"Our observation of our clients is that they all have a high tolerance for risk, they are just loss adverse. That can be a difficult expectation to manage."*

that is exceptionally large. This may work for insurance companies who have the "Law of Large Numbers" on their side, but when you are working with one single client, you only have a sample group of one.

Consequently we have had to tweak our view of modern portfolio theory to say, "Yes, we like the idea of multiple asset strategies, but we need to be able to avoid catastrophic losses." So during extreme volatile times, like we are seeing now, we need to have a predetermined strategy to minimize losses. Our strategy will not have us sell high all the time, nor will it have us buy low all the time. The goal is that we will be able to keep the volatility at a much lower clip for our clients and thereby give them a smoother experience and a higher probability of not running out of money.

Q. What does your average work week look like?
A. Every day is different, but it revolves around a few basic activities. One of them is talking to clients. Two would be answering emails. Three would be problem solving for clients. From 8:00 a.m. to 5:00 p.m. I am heavily involved in the business. About two nights a week I am answering emails from home. In terms of flexibility, as long as I have my Blackberry and the Internet, I can stay connected to my clients. Do I fully disconnect while I'm on vacation? Yes, so long as I answer emails when my wife isn't looking!

Q. What would you qualify as your most successful marketing strategy?
A. It is probably two-fold: First, providing such a great experience for our clients that it is easy and natural for them to tell their friends and family about us. Referrals are our primary source of business. The second strategy is Bob. By partnering with a CFP who is 30 years my elder, we can present to prospective clients a financial advising team that will be here for now and the next 40 years. I have heard the statistic that advisors will do business with people plus or minus 10 years

within their own age. Consequently, by having a business partner in his 60's, makes it a lot easier to work with clients who have the most need and motivation for retirement and estate planning.

Q. How tough do you think the first three years were for you as a planner?

A. In terms of toughness, the first three years weren't all that bad because I was in an administrative role. The hardest part was balancing the demands of trying to work a full-time schedule while attending school full-time. It was a great time to be in the business because I was already learning so many new things. I know a lot of firms use their rookies and interns to do cold calling and learn the business development side of the business first. I feel very fortunate because I started off doing financial planning and working with clients one on one. That hands-on training was invaluable because it exposed me to the issues we deal with and the impact we can have in a client's life.

Q. When you look at your personal situation, what is your view of retirement?

A. It's interesting, I heard a statistic that said roughly a third of retirees want to retire so they can truly retire and kind of check out. The next third take a cruise and then they wind down over time and they are content with that. Then there's the remaining third that are the re-inventors where they view retirement as an opportunity to try something new. Maybe volunteer full-time or try a second or third career. I would see myself falling into that third rung where retirement would almost be a rebirth into doing stuff you really want to. The best part about it is that I love what I am doing and assuming that I'm healthy, could continue to be in financial planning.

Q. What is your succession strategy? Is it to sort of continue down the line, or would you look to monetize the business and sell it as an asset and take that as part of your retirement package?

A. Probably a little bit of both. With most advisors over the age of 50, I think the next 10-20 years is a great time to look at the succession plan. In our firm, we welcome older advisors who want to continue their practice, but make sure that they have a succession plan in place. This acquisition strategy appears to be a great way to grow. Then I can bring on additional partners to help manage the books of business and grow the practice further. Moreover, as partners, we would be each other's succession plans as well!

> *"I may thank him for opening client's eyes as to how important it is that they understand who is managing their money."*

Q. If you had the chance to spend time with Bernie Madoff, what would you tell him?

A. I really don't know what I would tell him. I may thank him for opening client's eyes as to how important it is that they understand who is managing their money. We have a number of protections in place for our client's benefits – most of which they don't understand. As a result of Bernie, they are much more cognizant of their money and their advisor.

Q. If there was one thing you could change in the industry, what would it be?

A. It would be basic practice standards, and levels of certification. For example, look at the medical field. In order for somebody to be a surgeon, they have to go through a number of years of education, residency, and then certification. Only after a physician has proven his/herself, is he/she allowed to practice. As you pointed out, some of these brokers get a Series 7 without any education or training. They are then sent out to sell products to consumers. It's like hand-ing a baby a loaded gun. I think practice standards would be huge in advancing our industry to being considered more of a professional industry.

Q. Is there anything else that you would like to add to this? Anything that I haven't covered or a question I haven't asked?
A. I think this is a great industry for younger up and coming planners who are willing to put the work into it. It's a shame that there aren't as many people looking into this industry for career opportunities. I think if they are willing to take the time and learn the craft, it's a wonderful industry to work in.

21

"We are a very underserved field, not only for the number of people that need assistance, but also the number of people that are providing assistance."
Darin Shebesta, Jackson Financial Advisors

Darin Shebesta, at the age of 26, is a relative new comer to the industry. He has quickly established himself professionally and as a peer leader in the community, as a mentor and advocate for his fellow "younger" planners. Along with a few close associates, he established The Young Financiers in Chandler, Arizona. It is a group of young planners for young planners where experiences and advice can be shared. Darin's first position in the industry was as an intern in an analytical role with Northwestern, following graduation. Today, Darin works with Jackson Financial as an associate planner and sees himself as being in the right place at the right time for all the right reasons.

Q. Did you have aspirations to be a financial planner when you were at school?

A. I did not. It really came to me about a couple years out of school. The first day of my classes I was in the architecture school. When I went into the design class, they said something about, "Let's say there's oil that's spilled on the sand. What are you going to do about that?" I was just like, "Boy, I am not into this at all," and right then, at that moment, I switched over to business. So it was just completely not interesting to me on that side of things. So I said, "Well, business, money, let's move in that direction." I graduated with an undergraduate degree in finance at Arizona State University in the W.P. Carey School of Business at the age of 22.

Q. How did you formulate the role you are in now? How did you come to know the firm you are in currently?

A. After leaving college I got involved with a Financial Planning Association. I got to meet other planners across the valley. The more I met them and learned about what they did, I thought, "Wow, that's intriguing to me." Where I was we didn't get to interact with the clients; we only focused on the model portfolio, so we didn't get to deal with any of the other planning issues, and I felt kind of confined there. So during that time, I started researching these other advisory firms around town, I started running into younger and younger planners. I got to a point where there was maybe half a dozen I identified and I basically reached out to them all and I said, "What if we work together and form a group where we talk about what is going on in our fields, what's going on in our practices?" At this time, I was the only one who wasn't a planner in our group. It was called The Young Financiers, and currently there are about 40 individuals in Phoenix that fit the demographic of 36 and under that can take part in the group. Through this group I was introduced to Jackson Financial and decided to make the move to being a planner.

Q. What is your greatest motivation for being a planner today?
A. I have this burning desire to be able to work with people, not only in their financial lives, but it really drips down into their entire life. The financial is such a big piece of it and to be able to have that kind of impact and give them that guidance and direction lights me up.

Q. How much focus and emphasis and expectation do you have on financial reward?
A. It's one of those things where if I do what I love the money will come. I know that down the road I am going to be compensated. Right now, as long as I have got food on the table and a roof over my head and reliable transportation, I am willing to stick it out. I know that over time that's just how this business works; you just have got to get over the accumulation period, and then all of the sudden you have something significant.

Q. What do you see as being the greatest challenge in meeting client needs?

A. I feel like if you can adapt to "Who moved my cheese" concept, then there should not be a concern about the regulations. If you are doing what is right for the client, maybe you have to follow some more protocols, you will still be able to help clients. So the government is not going to dissuade me from helping clients. But I would say probably the biggest challenge is just sorting through information. There's just so much out there, with all the products and services available. The key is customizing it and doing all your due diligence so you can really say confidently, "I have looked at the alternatives and this is the best route we should take."

Q. In your practice do you manage your own portfolios or are you managed by third-party money managers?

A. We actually do a little bit of that. We used to do pretty much all with third party managers, and what happened was the managers weren't pulling their weight and they weren't very responsive when we needed to make changes, so we brought more of it back in-house. The downside is that it takes time away from looking at the big picture. I mean, we may be able to tell clients that we are monitoring their portfolios closely, making adjustments with the pull of a trigger, but I think that takes some resources from actually looking away at other planning issues that may in fact have a greater impact than making a percent or two more a year.

Q. When you are with a new client, somebody that is in the early stages of their career, what is the most important piece of advice you can provide?

A. Start acting right now versus pushing it off any further. They need to see the impact of starting sooner rather than later, that it really affects them and they say, "Wow, look at the difference that makes if I start at this time, if I contribute this amount." So time is really on their side where not everybody can say that. I also think what is important is being able, for them, to clarify and actually state the goals that are important to them because if they don't have them written down and they don't have them in concrete, then it's almost like a carrot on a stick. So that's important too, keeping them accountable to the goals they set.

Q. Do you find your peer clients receptive to your advice?
A. Well, I guess it depends. By the way, our practice works with a lot of clients that tend to be in the distribution phase of their lives. There hasn't been a ton of experience in working with people my age and that brings me to another point. With the way the industry is currently structured, we cannot effectively service that younger group of people. I am not sure the compensation structure is appropriate. It's a challenge to balance time and compensation and service levels.

Q. What is the greatest challenge facing the industry?
A. Trying to figure out what we are. I would really like to think that we are a profession, but you can't say that all financial services people are part of a profession because they are all not credentialed the same way. We need to figure out who does what, instead of muddying the waters with the consumers. Consumers are so confused with who does what and at what level.

Q. What frustrates you the most?
A. I am frustrated that we are not seen at the same level as CPAs and attorneys yet. I'd like to think we've got the skill set to be there, but there are just so many external forces. We really want to be that trusted advisor for the client I think as a whole, and I kind of have to say that I think CPAs probably have that hat as well as maybe some attorneys, they are seen probably as more professional, but I think we are working on that. It's just the frustration to know, "Okay, this is where I know we are going to be but we are not there yet and what does it take to get there? How long will that take?"

Q. What would you tell a college graduate with a degree in finance considering your chosen career?
A. Well, what's interesting about that is I told you I got a finance degree from the business school at ASU. It was corporate finance. They taught me how to go work for an Intel or a Boeing in the department running financial models. I would say that that's really not a whole lot of what we do over here. There are a lot of communication skills, there's a lot of that personal skill that you don't necessarily get in the finance curriculum. There are actually undergraduate, graduate degrees and PhD degrees in financial planning across the country. If I would have known about those programs, I would probably have leaned towards going to one of them because that would have satisfied my education requirement and then I could have sat for CFP exam right out of school. But somebody that did have a finance degree and was looking for advice on it, I would say, "Well, I think you have the quantitative skills of what it takes; now it's about brushing up on the personal or the communication skills."

Q. Do you feel the industry is overly complicated and products too many or too few?
A. Well, that was part of my comment before about having to filter through all the pertinent information. For example, we have been looking at these living benefits on these variable annuities. There's like several companies that are in the hunt and the devil is in the details. So to go in and discover how it works and really turning apples and oranges to apples and apples, that to me takes some extra work and it kind of seems crude, but then again, I guess you have competition and capitalism out there.

Q. The current situation in our economy and in the market has been fairly severe. How do you qualify it, whether it be detrimental or advantageous, when talking to a new investor, an established investor, or a retiree?
A. I think the retirees can definitely be scared, as their major

earning years have passed and they are relying on those funds for the rest of their life. So to take what they have accumulated over that period and have it apply for the time it took to accumulate, that's certainly a task. This idea with the younger people about being hesitant to get in or not, time is actually on your side. Markets are going to do what they are going to do, but if you don't train yourself to get started and be consistent about your contributions and keep doing what you need to do, you just keep pushing it off and that thing that you had on your side, time, is now further from helping you out.

Q. Has yours or the firm's investment style changed in the last three years?

A. We have taken the approach that there may not be one right way, but let's be on multiple horses. For example, some of the portfolios we can have it be a passive strategy, whether that's index or something related to DFA. Another strategy we may have some kind of alternative manager that is able to go in and out with full discretion. We may hold some companies that are active but they have to stay invested. So we have taken a different manager approach and said, "Okay, we don't know which one of these is going to be the best, but if we put some with each, you are going to have some success over the long term with those strategies because one of them is bound to out-perform."

Q. What does your average work week look like personally?

A. I am typically in about 7:30am and I leave about 5:00pm. But when you love what you do the time just really moves and when you are getting things done, you don't worry about, "Oh, when is it 5:00?" In terms of the type of stuff that goes on, my role at the firm is really one of a relationship manager, so when some of our clients call in I am the main point of contact and I can identify from there if their request is something that I am able to assist them with. Maybe it's something operational, whether it's getting a check or logging online to see their statement or something, but it might even be more of a planning type of question. If it's something I am not able to assist them with, then, we can bring Jared in, who is our senior planner. He definitely has the experience to solve pretty much any planning issue I have ever seen. Then we have Bob as our chief investment officer and our business development guru. I am also assisting with some marketing ventures, whether that be meeting the local businesses in the area, helping Bob facilitate a networking group that we do once a month, or putting on client events. With our planning software, I was the liaison to bring all of our clients on board to the new software when I first started working here. That's pretty much been implemented fully with all of our clients and when we bring a new client to the firm I can help them get set up on that platform.

Q. What do you consider to be the most successful marketing strategy that you have ever seen or ever experienced?
A. I really like the idea of getting to know the professionals. So with this group that Bob has going, Preferred Partners, they have a CPA, an estate planning attorney, mortgage broker, a residential commercial realtor, payroll person, real estate attorney and a divorce attorney. When you get a bunch of these white collared professionals together, I think our clients run in a lot of the same circles, whether they use these people for their occupations or they may be friends of these people, but where you get together consistently, you share about what's going on in your field and you are able to get to know other professionals so that you feel comfortable introducing them to other clients and what not. Word of mouth is really the strongest marketing tool because it builds so much rapport just by that introduction.

Q. You have been in the business six years, how tough were the first three years?
A. I interned at Northwestern Mutual. I think that was crucial to help me get out of my shell and basically call anybody and

get out there. There has to be that point where you've just got to put yourself out on the ledge and deal with the rejection piece, it is huge, if you can get over that sooner rather than later it's a big help. So if somebody wants to learn those sales skills, they can certainly get that at the Merrill's, the Northwestern's, that sort of thing. However working for those places, they are pretty much in a commission environment and eat what they kill whereas an environment like ours, its' very consultative, like a doctor's office. You learn by observing and there's not this go out and be in the acquisition phase. So, I would say that Northwestern was absolutely difficult, just because it was such a new perspective; it was a different environment than I had ever been in before in terms of just having to run your own business. Nobody is telling you what to do. You've got to dictate your own schedule in order to bring money in the door.

Q. What is your personal view of retirement?
A. I think it's one of those things where you do not have to ask, "Can we afford to do this?" It's like, "would we have fun doing this? Would we like to do this? Alright, let's go for it," instead of saying, "Well, how is that going to dangerously impact our financial well being." It's being able to do what we want, when we want that's pretty important. The freedom of the time is pretty significant, but along with the time, if we want to go somewhere, we don't have to ask anybody but ourselves. Not having to have the money be the top priority is the key.

Q. So, at the time you retire, 2040, is it your goal and aspiration to be the managing partner of the firm?
A. Absolutely. Jared is probably going to be retired already and so then there will be a whole new slew of people that are working with us. So it's funny, I haven't gotten to visualize that just yet because I think the first step is getting a piece of the company. I mean, not getting it, but earning it or paying for it.

Q. If you had the opportunity to talk to Bernie Madoff, what would you tell him?
A. If you can believe it or not, there would be no need for yelling. I would basically state that it's too bad you can't go back and undo what you did because you created a lot of ripples around the world, and we are having to work a little bit harder because of you. So I hope you found it was worth it because you are pretty much going to be stuck to this four grey walls area for the rest of your time.

Q. If there was one thing you could change in the industry, what would it be?
A. I would like to have it as an option at every university and college for there to be a curriculum for financial planning to give students the opportunity to choose that from the get-go.

Q. Do you have any last comments, suggestions, or observations of the industry?
A. I think we are a very underserved field, not only for the number of people that need assistance, but also the number of people that are providing assistance. I think it's just such a stellar opportunity. I think it may very well be the most fulfilling profession available out there, the satisfaction, the compensation, the flexibility, the notoriety. I am so excited for the future of what this brings and you can talk regulation all day, but I still think there are so much more greater things that are going to happen for the better. I am just looking forward to spending my career, and my life, dedicated to this.

"Our calling is the point at which our deepest gladness meets the world's deepest need."

-Frederick Buechner

22

"When something that comes along is not in your focus area, you have to pass on it."
   Gerald Steffes, Steffes Financial, LTD

Gerald Steffes has been in the financial planning industry for 20 years. He is a CPA and worked in public accounting for four years prior to becoming a CFP. Leaving his accounting career behind in 1988, Gerald worked for Financial Planning Partners, Ltd., a Lincoln National Life subsidiary, for seven years. Gerald is now the owner of Steffes Financial, Ltd, a Registered Investment Advisor. He has one other advisor, Amy White, CFP, and two administrative assistants. They currently manage or consult on approximately $150M of assets. They consist of $90M private client and $60M 401(k) assets.

Q. Was a career in financial planning a childhood ambition of yours going through school?
A. No. When I was growing up my father ran a small business and therefore I always planned to run my own business someday. I attended Kansas State University with a focus on business classes. In college I pursued an accounting degree as I figured that would be the best way to learn how other people actually run a successful business. After graduation and four years in public accounting, I finally started my own business.

Q. What is your greatest motivation for being a planner today?
A. I really enjoy working with all my clients. I have become good friends with almost all my clients and really enjoy our client meetings. Most of my client meetings run a full two hours, even though consultants to our industry say, "You've got to get those meetings down to one hour." I just spend too much time talking to my clients; I enjoy it.

Q. What do you see as being the greatest challenge in meeting your client needs?

A. Making smarter business decisions when it comes to their investment portfolio so that they have enough retirement capital to retire. The bottom line is the client is relying on us for their financial security and we have got to continue to learn and make smarter decisions. We have tried to contract out the investment portfolio management but after trying several different firms, we found the cost to the client did not justify their performance.

Q. When you have a young client what would be the most important piece of advice that you offer them?

A. I think the most important thing we tell all our 401(k) participants is get signed up in your 401(k) or 403(b) for at least a 4% deferral and then every January raise it 1%. If married, have your spouse do the same thing every year at their work until you are both at a 10% deferral. Whatever the company puts in as a match or profit-sharing contribution is excess on top of what you do. That is probably the single most important financial advice I could give a young couple. You still have to do the life insurance, buy a house, the car, keep the credit card paid off, all that stuff. But paying yourself first in your 401(k) plan is job one. Everything else will take care of itself.

> *"When something that comes along is not in your focus area, you have to pass on it."*

Q. What is the greatest challenge that you see facing our industry today?

A. Financial regulations. We need financial regulation to prevent fraud and protect the public, however some of it is too extreme, so there's got to be a better balance of financial regulation.

Q. What frustrates you the most about the industry?

A. Complexity. In every business there exists a ceiling of complexity. As financial advisors we try to do everything. As our practices grow, we eventually get to the point where we hit a ceiling on our production. To break through this ceiling of complexity we need systems and support. It is critical we develop systems and build a support team that enhances the value to our clients.

Q. Is this complexity a necessary evil of the work we do?
A. I believe it is. This is a very complex industry and to be honest with you, it's a barrier of entry to the industry for people that just think they are going to walk in here and make a lot of money and sell stuff. In addition, there are too many advisors in our industry with no credentials. I would love to see regulations regarding the credentials needed to call yourself a financial advisor.

Q. What would you tell a college graduate who has a degree in finance and is considering your chosen career?
A. I would say it's a great industry, but like everything else, it takes dedication, a lot of hours and tenacity to build a practice. If you can be mentored by somebody for two or three years, it's well worth it. The best way is to go with somebody who is already systematized, so learn their systems and build off of their success.

Q. Do you feel that the industry is overly complicated and the number of products are too many?
A. Yes, choice is good and it benefits financial advisors, as clients need our expertise to figure out what's best for their situation. This also can lead to financial advisors trying to specialize in too many areas.

Q. If you could, how would you change that? What aspect would you cut back on or modify?
A. Bottom line, you can't do everything for everyone. You've got to decide, "What is my expertise?" When something that comes along is not in your focus area, you have to pass on it.

Q. Focus in on the significance of the last three years. Have the last three years has been advantageous or detrimental if you were a new investor, an established investor, or a retiree?

A. They have been detrimental to all investors and not just the last three years. The baby boom generation has actually been hard hit twice in the last ten years, from the 2000 tech decline and the 2008 banking crisis. I think it's been devastating on the retirement time horizon for the baby boom generation. It's moved everybody back five years, if not more. For advisors, it's been a plus as more clients seek financial counsel.

Q. Has the events of the last three years effected the ways you manage money?

A. Yes. Following or during the tech decline of 2000, we started being more of an "active asset allocator." We don't just buy and hold. When I first got into the business, everything was buy and hold. Look at the Morningstar research; get the highest rate mutual fund, buy and hold.

With the banking crisis of 2008, we actually started a core and satellite approach to asset allocation. With the core allocation we use strategic asset allocation, which is basically a diversified buy and hold approach. The satellite allocation is more tactical where we are going to watch the trends and be more active with it. In this global economy and with the significant events we have seen in the last ten years, I am not convinced buy and hold is the right thing to do.

Q. What does your average work week look like in terms of hours spent, hours on the business, hours in the business?

A. We do what is called time blocking and we try to have two appointments in the morning and two in the afternoon. I don't do evening meetings anymore, so the last meeting starts at 4:00pm. I typically get home by 6:30pm. That's Monday through Thursday. Friday's are reserved for my buffer days where I catch up and do special projects.

Q. What would you consider your most successful marketing strategy?

A. What launched my career was a CPA breakfast club. In the non-tax season, I sponsored a breakfast for CPA's once a month for seven months. We faxed an invitation to area CPA's and attorneys for a 2 hour continuing education program and breakfast. We charged $10 to cover our cost and then lined up qualified speakers. We would speak once a year on a financial planning topic.

We never asked for referrals. We would however send a letter each tax season offering support on any financial planning question the CPA may be asked by their clients. We would also send the largest "Crunch" candy bar in the envelope with a letter stating it's "Crunch Time," right before tax season with my business card. The candy bar pretty much insured they would open the envelope and read our letter.

> "I would like to see some regulations on who can call themselves a financial planner."

Q. How difficult would you say the first three years as a planner were for you?

A. I was actually very disappointed in how slow and difficult it was to build my practice; I thought we would build it faster since I was already a CPA. Wrong. Then we finally got to a point where all of a sudden things were clicking. Referrals started coming in and we focused on building systems.

Q. What is your personal view of retirement?

A. I am currently 49 and would like to be able to semi-retire by age 60. I do not anticipate ever selling my practice; I plan to coast into retirement, taking care of my key clients and get down to one assistant.

Q. So would you see Amy taking over the clients that you ultimately don't have the time or desire to continue to manage?

A. Amy White currently helps on my 401(k) plans and already engages those prospects who do not meet my $500,000 asset minimum.

Q. If you had a chance to talk to Bernie Madoff, what would you tell him?
A. How disappointed I am in him. Hopefully the hedge fund industry incurs a little more SEC oversight to prevent the next Bernie Madoff.

Q. If there was one thing you could change in the industry, what would it be?
A. I would like to see some regulations on who can call themselves a financial planner. I think the CFP is going in the right direction. I just think there should be a credential and minimum education requirements similar to if you want to be a CPA or a physician.

23

"Advisors are still entrepreneurs, it's just that generation X and Y are very clear about what they like to do and they are willing to pay somebody else to do what they don't like to do."
Amy Webber, Cambridge Investment Research, Inc.

Amy Webber is president and chief operating officer at Cambridge Investment Research, Inc. With over 23 years industry experience, Amy's comprehensive executive management expertise includes leadership in compliance, finance, human resources, marketing, operations, service, and technology. Amy's executive accomplishments include significant initiatives – such as the implementation of a complete virtual office technology platform, the 2009 launch of a comprehensive wealth management platform, and the formation of the Cambridge New Century Council - a unique initiative intended to draw on the insights of 40-something advisors to define the tools and infrastructure needed to serve clients in need of wealth management and financial planning guidance in the next 10-20 years. Based on her work with the New Century Council, Amy recently spearheaded the launch of an industry-leading social networking pilot program designed to meet the interests of Cambridge advisors while appropriately observing regulatory guidelines regarding client communications. Additionally, she completed the Securities Industry Institute's Executive Program at the Wharton School of Business. Wealth Manager magazine recognized her as one of the "Top 50 Women in Wealth Management" in 2009 and 2010. Amy resides in Fairfield, Iowa, with her husband, Matt, and their two children and is actively involved in the community through various board and volunteer associations.

Q. How did you come to be involved in financial services in general?

A. When I was 18, I went to Madison Business College in Madison, Wisconsin. They have classes in the morning and an internship program in the afternoon. I started in an entry-level position at a broker-dealer in September of 1987, so when the crash happened that October, while I still had absolutely no idea what was going on, I was in the midst of it and it got into my blood. Other than a very brief, one-year period, I have not left the back office of an independent broker-dealer. That was 23 years ago. I basically worked my way up from that point forward.

Q. Was that college chosen specifically to allow you to enter this market?

A. It was coincidental. I had absolutely no idea when I was 18 what I wanted to do when I grew up. Business certainly, but in what way I was not sure. The broker-dealer I went to work for initially was a very small husband and wife team that believed in our industry so passionately that they really made it a point to bring in young people. I think it is people like that, even today, that will make sure that financial services continue to thrive. We have to think about the next generation and they did that for me and took a risk on me, which hopefully paid off for the both of us. I stayed with them for seven years and left only due to a relocation.

Q. Did you go straight from Madison to Cambridge?

A. No. I moved to Phoenix. I worked for about four years for Sun America Securities, which was AIG Advisors and is now Sagepoint. There I met my husband and decided to come back to the Midwest, at which point, I was introduced to Eric Schwartz and joined Cambridge. I was employee number 22 at Cambridge. I joined in April 1998. Total revenues the prior year were approximately $7M and we are going to be close to $340M this year. That was between 1997 and today.

Q. As the COO of an independent broker-dealer, what does your day look like?

A. I am the president and COO; Eric is the CEO and chairman. I call myself the chief culture officer more than I do any of the other titles that I carry. Everything except marketing and recruiting reports to me and has reported to me for about the last ten years. As the chief culture officer, I have surrounded myself with phenomenal people for the past 13 years. I don't spend a lot of time in the day-to-day; I do spend a lot of time making sure that our culture doesn't change with the type of growth we've had. I don't believe that a company's culture has to change simply because they have grown. We have had significant growth in those 13 years, but I don't know how many other CEOs or presidents or even senior executives spend the amount of time that I do managing corporate culture. I still personally meet with all new employees to talk about our values, our industry, who we are and what we want to maintain, who our clients are – who the end client is – and that we are doing our part to help the end client meet their financial goals and dreams. That is why we continue to grow and are having the success that we have. All of us, at the senior level, have not gotten so distracted with other priorities that we forget how important that is, and we do spend time focusing on those culture issues.

> *"I believe that it isn't in anyone's best interest in the future to be out there by themselves; it's not in their best interest and it's not in their clients' best interest."*

Another significant tool to maintain culture is personal contact at senior levels. I have a tremendous amount of contact with our clients, the rep/advisors, to ensure that we are doing what we need to be doing to support them in the growth of their businesses.

I kind of look at our associates here as an extension of our clients and if they are happy, that turns into happy end clients. But if we quit paying attention to it, the growing pains could then take over. Now, I have to admit that in the last five years, I spend more time on compliance and regulatory issues than I wish I had to, but the industry demands it. Ten years ago you would sit in a room full of presidents and CEOs and they would be talking about exciting things like innovation, marketing, and business building. We have had to work really hard the last year or two to get back to some of that, because for awhile we were consumed with regulation and compliance issues. We still are, but we all realize that it's the world we live in today and if we don't get back to thinking about the other aspects, we aren't going to continue to thrive.

Q. When you look at the independent channel as a whole, what do you see as its major challenges as opposed to the wire houses and insurance companies?

A. I think we have to continue to educate and differentiate ourselves in the eyes of the investing public and the regulators, and that's going to be a challenge. Many people do not recognize what independence is or means. A lot of things have happened over the last couple years that have splashed on all of us – the broad financial services industry – and we have to continue to do a better job of explaining who we are. You hear the phrase "unintended consequences" all the time, and it's going to keep happening to us if we don't lobby for ourselves and get out there. We do a lot of that here at Cambridge through the Financial Services Institute (FSI). They really are, by far, our loudest voice, but there are lots of other things going on as well. We spend a lot of time educating official agencies, when we have the chance, as to what a true independent channel means.

Profitability is challenging. Through regulation, we see various threats to the broker-dealer model, particularly independent broker-dealers. Interestingly enough, I think even the term broker-dealer isn't completely relevant anymore.

> *"I don't spend a lot of time in the day-to-day; I do spend a lot of time making sure that our culture doesn't change with the type of growth we've had."*

I think we at Cambridge have transformed ourselves into more than a broker-dealer. To some offices we are a technology provider, to other offices we are a compliance and regulatory consultant. Our whole initiative in the next few years is specifically designed around identifying things that are on an advisor's P&L where they are spending money. We want to leverage our scale and our expertise to deliver services to them for less, thus making ourselves indispensible as a true partner. It's not just about being a broker-dealer anymore; it is a relationship business, and that's a challenge for some broker-dealers. I think we are definitely out in the front. I see the younger generations pushing us to be that clearing house of outsourcing for them, whatever that may be. I have been challenged by some older advisors that I am describing a revised version of a wire house, so if the next generation of advisors wants the broker-dealer to do everything for them, why wouldn't they just join a wire house? The difference is the younger advisors want to outsource, but they want choices in what to outsource. Advisors are still entrepreneurs, it's just that generation X and Y are very clear about what they like to do and they are willing to pay somebody else to do what they don't like to do.

Q. Does Cambridge compensate for the loss in the revenue streams that are being regulated away with these additive consulting services?

A. This is yet to be determined. I think if we pick the right services we can, and that's the trick. We are doing studies right now and we have gotten some ideas that appear to have some legs, but what we've got to prove to ourselves, through pilot testing later in 2011, is whether or not we can really do it for less than they are doing it. That's going to be the main driver. In some cases, it may not have to be less, but it definitely has to be better or less.

Q. So, you mentioned consulting as an opportunity and that's very specific to Cambridge. Do you see opportunities for the channel as a whole?

A. As far as I can tell, there are only a couple others left in the truly independent space, so there are huge opportunities for the channel as a whole. Really, two, three, or four independent broker-dealers, mid-sized or large, that are left, are still truly independently owned. There is a degree of struggle in the smaller independents on whether or not they even want to stay in this business for lots of reasons. So, I think the opportunities are huge for the independent channel and for us to continue to grow. It goes back to that education I was talking about: how do we educate the advisors, who are not in the independent channel today, about why they should be? I am fiercely committed to the independent channel and I think it's what is best for the client in the end, but I do think there has been a threat to that model for lots of different reasons over time. We must do a better job of educating everybody on why we think it's a great model for the client.

Q. Do you see the Internet, and the availability of information, changing in the way in which the client and the advisor interact with one another over the coming years?

A. I am definitely starting to see a trend and some of this has to do with some of the younger generations. We see a situation where we could be interfacing more directly with the end client in the future. The challenge is figuring out how we do that without infringing on that sense of independence. That's the reason we haven't felt the demand to do it from our current advisor base, in large part because they typically want the client to know them as the primary relationship contact. But due to the upcoming generational differences, the demand is going to change. I think about things like our annual mailings and the unbelievable increase of required disclosures, and how the end client could have a unique ID and password for Cambridge five years down the road so they can access everything electronically from one place. We will try to do as much as we can on our end before that point, where end clients can get anything they need related to Cambridge, including all the current and potential disclosures that are coming at us. I think we need to be able to figure out how to integrate brokerage statements and confirms and prospectuses into this engine. I think that maybe there's a bit of a private label that's going to have to happen, in that the advisor is still in the front. So, I suspect five years from now we will absolutely have a client portal that gives them everything that they need. I don't see how we can't go that direction.

Q. Do you see more money flowing into the third-party platforms and the self-managed platforms?
A. Significant growth or movement from self-managed to third-party managed is not happening today at Cambridge. It's funny because there's a line of thought out there, and the media appears to believe it, that if the fiduciary standard goes through, everyone – all broker-dealers – will start to shut down the ability for advisors to do self-managed business and they will force everything into broker-dealer or third-party models. I don't know if we are unique, but that is one outsourcing option where the trend isn't as strong for us. Even these younger advisors that are coming in, let's face it, they are coming in under the wing of someone who has managed the client's assets themselves and it's very hard to change once the client accepts that role. There are some clients that are more open to it, but the transformation and adoption of the advisor as the "relationship trusted advisor" versus the "money manager" has not gone as quickly as we anticipated. I believe in third-party platforms and the outsourcing model – don't get me wrong. I think they are a great tool where it makes sense for the advisor and the client, but I don't know, at least in the next three to five years without

something more drastic happening, that it's going to be a huge movement.

Q. So five to ten years from now, where do you see the regulatory environment? Where you would like to see it?
A. What I would like to see, and it's going to happen, is a continued convergence of models [registered representative or investment advisor]. It will come down to the details, and there are a lot of things we can do wrong here, but what's best for the client is the elimination of all of this different hat-wearing confusion. The clients don't understand it. They don't have any idea whether or not their advisor is a rep or an advisor, and I think that it's best for everybody that uniform standards continue to take form.

Q. Do you believe that greater responsibility has to be pushed back onto the clients?
A. I believe it is reasonable to expect a certain amount of responsibility to be shouldered at the client level, but we need to take steps to make it as clear and easy to understand as possible. The client needs to understand they have a responsibility to do their own due diligence on the advisor they choose to do business with, and to read the material the advisor provides them with. Financial services are largely based on two-way trust between advisor and client. I would emphasize the importance of financial advisors recognizing and living up to the trust that the end client is placing in them as their advisor.

Q. So looking at the broker-dealers as a whole, you mentioned some of the regulatory environment is going to impinge upon revenue streams, how do you see the broker-dealer model evolving in the next three to five years?
A. Broker-dealers need to expand their offerings beyond what is expected of them today. I'm not suggesting that they can be everything to everyone, but I'm betting right now on the outsourcing model and that a true partner can leverage its

expertise to offer more than what most do today. It seems to me that there is some apprehension at the broker-dealer level about the so-called hybrid model, but the fact that 85% of our partners do both commissions and fees today tells me that it isn't going to go away. We have to find ways to add value to those practices. The reaction in the industry, because they don't know where the things are going and the uncertainty is so intimidating, is to lock things down. The successful ones, the ones that come out on the other end, are not going to do that.

Q. So when you boil all that back wrap technology as well into the same discussion, where do you see the sole-proprietor advisor being five years from now?

A. Not a sole proprietor, probably. I think we have to encourage the partnership and the ensemble models. I believe that it isn't in anyone's best interest in the future to be out there by themselves; it's not in their best interest and it's not in their clients' best interest. We know from the extensive work with succession planning and business continuity, that it's better for the advisor, the advisor's family, and their loved ones, if they start to think more about building something that can survive after they are gone in one way, shape, or form. And we know that it's better for the client. Some of the most successful ensemble models include both genders, because clients and investors aren't always going to connect with the same individual. Almost every day, I have conversations with some of our advisors who just found out that they have a health problem or that somebody in their family has a health problem that's going to distract them from the business and they are very concerned because there's no back up, no infrastructure. We find advisors are pretty open to the idea once you present the solution.

Q. Is the regulatory environment going to make it more difficult for the transfer of assets between advisors?

A. The regulatory environment is going to continue making it harder for those things to happen between firms, but most of the regulations are still at the broker-dealer level or the RIA level. That allows us more flexibility and control on behalf of the advisors if we are the broker-dealer or the RIA. We don't have a regulatory issue if we transfer accounts to another Cambridge advisor and provide personal information as long as we've disclosed we'll do so, because it's the broker-dealer level. All the more reason to get out and promote that a formal partnership has to be formed, and both advisors should be at the same place to make this process as seamless as possible.

Q. Do you agree that there should be a minimum standard for the term financial planner to be adopted? Do you think that should be the CFP?

A. I do agree that minimum standards are important, and it comes back to protecting the investor. I also believe that the regulatory environment demands protection of the investor. I support effective regulation, which does not necessarily mean new regulation. If the CFP is already out there and they can do it effectively without unintended consequences, I think that's okay.

Q. Do you believe there are enough women in the industry? You must have better visibility of this than most.

A. No, I don't. At Cambridge, 14% of the advisors are female. The percentage of women that are fund managers in the industry is more like 12%; in the financial services industry as a whole, you get down to something like 10%. I think that's really low. It's one of my interests. It's not about fewer men, but it is about more women. The investing public will be better served by having options. Not all women want to work with a woman, and not all men want to work with a man. We are not encouraging young women who can be very good planners, particularly because many women are natural caregivers and that caregiving side of us can make a great financial advisor. An ensemble that carries both genders in it, so that clients can go to who they naturally feel comfortable with, is the perfect world in my mind. So, I would like to figure out a way for Cambridge, or myself personally, to create an environment that promotes our industry to women.

Q. Can you see any financial incentives that could be provided to attract more women into the industry?
A. Not directly, but maybe indirectly. For instance, I am working with one of our female advisors to determine if there is value in forming a super-OSJ [office of supervisory jurisdiction], if you will, that specializes in growing, mentoring, and training female advisors. We are also investing in special initiatives this year geared towards helping women advisors, such as our Women Advisors Conference, formation and facilitation of an advisor-to-advisor peer group, and some technological solutions in the digital media realm.

Q. So what would you say to a woman that is looking to re-enter the workplace to steer them into our industry rather than realty, for example?
A. What I have discovered is that some women find it difficult, and are hesitant, to market themselves, particularly in our industry. Women have to learn how to promote and market themselves and talk about what they are good at. They have to go out and get some formal training to do that because most of us are raised not to talk about ourselves like that. I have heard a lot of speakers who say the reason there aren't enough women in financial services is because we don't promote math and sciences to women in school. There might be some truth to that, but I am not sure that's the biggest limitation. The biggest limitation is marketing and sales skills and like anything, sales have a huge upside potential if you are good at it. It's many of the same things that attract men to this business, but I think clients tend to talk to women more about their entire life situation, it's not just about money and the investment.

Women tend to navigate to similar careers in areas like real estate, so I would talk to them about the fact that while it's fulfilling to help a couple, a family, or an individual find their home, there is even more fulfillment in helping those same people meet their bigger picture financial goals.

The clients benefit from that caregiver quality that women often bring to the table and the female advisor achieves great emotional fulfillment from the role – a true win/win!

Q. Do you think women are more perturbed by the need to pass the license exams as a prerequisite to coming into the business?

A. The only frame of reference that I have for this question is here at Cambridge. We require 30-40% of our positions to be licensed, including everyone in management level positions. This was my decision, not an industry-wide rule. I believe to be credible and be part of our leadership team you need to do it. I have not seen any evidence that exams are any more intimidating for the women than they are for the men. It is a great accomplishment, but not a slam dunk and the individual certainly has to be committed.

Q. So at a personal level, what challenges have you faced specific to the fact that you are female and extremely successful?

A. I get this question all the time and I guess all I can say is I have been fortunate enough to not ever feel like being a female has gotten in my way. In my 23 years in this industry, I have only been with three companies, I was led by both male and female superiors, and none of them ever made me feel like that mattered. I have been an individual and I have been allowed to grow and flourish. I know it happens; I have heard the horror stories from others, but I have never bumped into it personally.

Q. In professional circles and events, do you get the sense of being treated differently?

A. Maybe a few times when I first meet people and shake their hand. I am intuitive enough that I can tell they would rather ask me to go get them coffee, but when I have the opportunity to open my mouth and speak, I watch that quickly change. I am not tooting my own horn there; I just don't let it stop me. I don't let it intimidate me; I move through it quickly. I think most of those people have females in their organization, even if they are not the president, which they do rely on. As soon as I open my mouth, they can tell that I have a level of intelligence and experience, so the fact that I am a woman goes away.

Q. Lastly, I know this is probably far off in your mind, but how do you consider retirement for you and your family?
A. Wow, this was the hardest question you have asked me – I don't know. I am 41. You're right; it does feel a long way off. At this stage in my life, I am totally consumed by what I love to do here, and then when I am home, I focus on spending time with my husband and my two children. That is fulfilling today. But I guess my dream for that next phase, when things naturally should slow down, is that I want to run to something, not from something. I have seen enough people who have been so afraid of retirement that it becomes a negative process, not a positive process, not moving onto the next thing. So that's what I want. Something very attractive to me would be something surrounding children. Maybe in my retirement I would have a ranch and an organization that I can be the leader of, an important part of, providing opportunities to children who haven't had the opportunities that my kids have had.

"The larger the problem you solve, the greater the rewards for solving it."

-Anonymous

24

"The need for independent financial planning has increased dramatically because of the turmoil in the marketplace."
Joel Weiner, Professional Training Services

Joel Weiner is a practicing certified financial planner (CFP) and has been working in the business for almost 30 years. Joel has experience as a practicing attorney for the last five years. Joel owns a training school and partners up with the CFP program at St. Paul University. He has experience in the insurance industry, brokerage industry, and now as an attorney, and educator.

Q. Which came first, the legal or the advisory?
A. Advisory. I have only been practicing law about five years now.

Q. I have to ask, what drove you to study law and take the bar?
A. I graduated law school in 1970, many years ago. Then about four and a half years ago it struck me, I have been in the financial industry most of my life, so I just decided it was something I hadn't done and I was going to go take the bar and then practice law.

Q. Which do you prefer?
A. Each one has its moments I guess. I do securities arbitrations and things like that which puts me right back in the industry anyway. I do the securities, but as it turns out, with the way the economy goes, most of my law practice is family law right now.

Q. When you look at financial planning, what's your general view? Do you think we are in a good place?
A. Well I may not be answering your question directly but I think

many people need financial planning. Probably more so now than anytime I can think of in the last 20-some odd years. The need for independent financial planning has increased dramatically because of the turmoil in the marketplace and because of the many, many, unethical people that have proven to be unethical in the industry over the years, i.e. Madoff, as well as many others.

Q. You specifically qualify the independent channel, is that because you don't feel the captive channel is as fair towards the planning as they are their product?

A. Well when I say independent, I mean independent financial advice versus a financial planner that may work for a brokerage firm. The advisor offer products, transactions, and collect commissions versus charging a financial plan fee strictly to do financial planning for an individual. They don't sell products. I am not talking about a registered investment advisor (RIA); I am talking about a fee-only financial planner module.

I feel strongly because I come from the other model. I do financial planning, I am with the brokerage side of the business, and I charge fees. If a client comes to me for financial planning, I will not charge them for a financial plan unless they don't do investing with me. I know I am going to get paid somewhere. I don't double dip them. What's happening now is you have more folks looking for that independent planning because they lack trust in general with people in the brokerage business, people doing transactions. Then of course, if you go into an area of an insurance company, you have a financial planner who only has products they can sell. Insurance, maybe annuities and maybe some mutual funds. The individual may feel they are not getting a fair shake

> *"I still believe that the average person looking for true financial planning advice (not the transactional side) is looking to get help because of what has gone on in our economy..."*

because of the limitation of that planner. That also tends to drive people towards looking for independent financial planning advice.

Q. What sort of challenges do you see they will face in the next three to five years?

A. I think the challenges that are being faced depend upon whether you are talking about a person that is new to this field. I think those challenges are going to be more so economic, such as, "How am I going to survive? How am I going to afford marketing? How am I going to afford to look for my next client?" Versus someone who has been in this business who already has a book of business, who already has established a work place and has an office or access to an office. I think that person's challenges will be, "How do I really want to deliver my financial planning services going forward? Am I going to go towards the fee-only side, be a little more independent, or am I going to stay mixed between financial planning and doing products? Will people really think they are getting independent advice?" They will have to go a step further with all the new security laws that will be forthcoming from the new National Securities Act and the new National Regulatory Agency. There's going to be more and more oversight, and that's going to be a challenge.

Q. Talking about the hybrid model, many RIAs also have a relationship with a broker dealer. Independent broker dealers have access to a very broad spectrum of product, do you see the broker-dealer community being challenged as this industry evolves?

A. It's kind of an interesting question because over the last few years we have seen major brokerage firms wanting to get their people to become CFPs. Now you are using the term "registered investment advisor" and I have to separate that totally from planning. So bear with me for a moment. We see brokerage firms wanting their registered reps to become CFPs because the brokerage firms are recognizing that the average person wants some financial planning advice beyond just going to a stock broker and getting recommendations as a result of everything that has been going on over the last few years.

Well now I am starting to see a change from that, and as an example let me elaborate. A major insurance company, just three years ago, had a major push to get their insurance people, those who were interested, to become CFPs, and made it financially rewarding to them if they did. Now, because of the new oversight coming and because of the word "fiduciary," that company has backed off and they don't want to be involved with having CFPs any longer. They are not making those recommendations. I am starting to see that with some large brokerage firms, where now they don't even want you to use the CFP designation on a business card because they are afraid of that oversight and the legal implications of being a fiduciary.

Q. By virtue of being a CFP, does that automatically create the fiduciary position with a client, or does it have to be qualified in the agreement with the client?

A. No, it's automatic now. This came into being almost a year ago. It's now automatic under the CFP board's code of ethics, and there are a number of CFPs who have left the industry because they don't want to do this because of, once again, potential future legal implications. That's making this business a little bit tougher. If you follow the news, when the new national security act just passed, there was a battle in congress over who would be a fiduciary or not. Well, they passed the law and in the same law, this new law, they gave the SEC six months to come up with the answer and told them to basically investigate it, form committees, and make a recommendation as to whether stock brokers, insurance agents, and on and on it goes, should rise to the level of fiduciary as are currently CFPs, and by the way RIAs.

Q. Do you see a situation which is either advantageous or disadvantageous for the new generation who are more academically oriented by virtue of CFP classes, financial degrees etc, versus the older generation where most have come through the insurance business?

A. That's a tough one because I guess it would depend more on a client. As an example, you've got to say to yourself, "Who really looks for financial planning?" Well, your typical person would be a couple in their 50's. They are thinking, "I am going to have to retire one day and I would like to get that financial advice." So they go visit and interview a financial planner who is 23 years old. Good luck. That's going to be the problem for the young, new financial planner because your person in their 50's, in their mind are saying, "You are too young; you don't have any experience because you are too young, and I don't care how much you know academically, you don't get it yet." You are going to see a lot of that. That's going to be one of your potential problems for your new, younger, just graduating, well educated people who now become a financial planner.

> *"There are a lot of people out here who call themselves financial planners and they don't have a clue about financial planning."*

Now, on the other hand, what you really need to look at is who is coming into the financial planning industry? In our training school, with St. Paul and the training we do for persons going to take the CFP 10-hour exam, the majority of those persons are older people who either had another career, like a CPA or attorneys. But the majority of them are older people who have been in financial services, either the insurance industry or stock broker industry. Now here's the dilemma for them; coming to that 50 year old couple, no question the planner has the experience and has the right age. That's not a problem, but then you get the question, "Well Mr. CFP, how long have you been a CFP?" "Oh gee, I passed the test three months ago and here I am." That may be a problem, of course.

I still believe that the average person looking for true financial planning advice (not the transactional side) is looking to get help because of what has gone on in our economy and what has gone on in newspapers with all these nasty, bad people out there getting arrested. We all know it's a small number of people that are the problem, but unfortunately the press only broadcasts the small number of bad guys. They never write articles about the good people in this business.

Q. What are things that you feel should change in order to make our industry a better industry?

A. I think that more CFPs need to change their model a little bit and make sure that their business is ethics friendly. The line that they need to think of all the time is, "Do what is in the best interest of the client. Period." And in fact, under the National Reform Act that just passed, that was one of the major slogans that got written into the law – "Do what is in the best interest of the client." This is common sense, but sometimes it's not with our everyday planners. For reasons such as, "I am having a bad month financially and I need to make more money," "I work for a Merrill-Lynch of the world and they don't want me to make the disclosures that I am suppose to make according to my CFP code of ethics." Sometimes people in those businesses have to make a career decision: "Am I going to do it the right way? If my boss and that large bank or that brokerage firm doesn't want to let me do it, then I need to make a career change." That's going to be another challenge out here. We do "ethical presentations" at our training schools across the country for CFPs, and in Illinois for insurance people because there is now a required law that says they have to.

Q. In general terms, do you see the number of CFP students in your classes who are younger than 30 years of age increasing or decreasing?

A. Actually, it's about the same. There are probably 35% under 30. I think there are less people getting into this industry now and more people leaving the industry than ever before.

Q. Do you think that's predominantly because of regulation and oversight along with this whole fiduciary thing?

A. Absolutely. I will tell you something else. The CFP boards are a little bit out of control too. Since they moved to Washington they are becoming more regulatory in their thought processes and the average planner is getting a little bit upset, and I know many people who have left because they can't deal with all these regulations. You need regulation; no one is challenging that, but everyone is going overboard right now. What is going to happen with this new National Regulatory Agency is more layers of problems. Quite frankly, if I came into this industry today, and understood what was going on, I would not be a financial planner. I would probably not even be in a financial services industry. It's just not worth it.

Q. What sort of conversations do you have with your students? Are they typically bullish about their careers or are they doing a CFP because their employer expects it of them? Are they, in the majority, self-employed or employed people?

A. The majority of them are looking for more money, let's lay it right on the line here – they are looking for another niche. They are having problems surviving as an insurance agent or just a regular stock broker. There are some companies that they are getting pressure from to become CFPs for all the reasons I discussed earlier, but the majority of them are getting into this business to find a financial niche in which they can get a better economic future for themselves.

Q. Do you think there needs to be a minimum academic requirement such as a CFP to qualify to use the designation "Financial Planner"?

A. Well yes. I have been saying that for a lot of years. There are a lot of people out here who call themselves financial planners and they don't have a clue about financial planning. Who can use the term financial planning? Unfortunately the National Security Act started to address it, but then I think they dropped the ball on it. You can take a person out here who sells life insurance and they are calling themselves financial planners. You take a client who doesn't have a clue about this industry, some guy says I am a financial planner, so what's the naïve client going to think? "Well, this guy is probably giving me good stuff," and that's far from the truth. That's just absolutely nonsense. But, that is a problem. I think there has to be a separation.

"It's not a sprint; it's a marathon."
Keith Wetjen, APW Wealth Advisors

Keith Wetjen is 37 years old and a lawyer. While in law school he became interested in securities and insurance. He committed himself to taking the needed licenses and exams while in school. Keith is also a CFP. He has been involved in the business for 10 years and has two partners in the firm. They manage $200M assets and consider themselves to be holistic planners primarily for business owners and senior corporate executives.

Q. Did you always desire to be in the financial planning arena, or was this a surprise to you?
A. I didn't always want to get into financial planning. I had always wanted to be in business for myself. I have a law degree and my primary purpose of going to law school was to position myself best so I could put my best foot forward with what I decided to do, and when I was in law school it just so happened that the direction I started taking was in the financial planning and insurance related areas. I found that I liked those particular areas. I got out of law school, passed the bar, and got into the financial planning profession.

Q. What was it particularly that drew you towards it while you were in law school?
A. The subject matter, the opportunity to be independent, to be my own boss, to find a way to help the most amounts of people with an area I enjoyed.

Q. What do you qualify as your single greatest motivation today for being a planner?
A. The opportunity to help people, the ability to stay independent, work for myself, and be entrepreneurial.

Q. What do you see as being the greatest challenge, in meeting client expectations?

A. The continuing goal of trying to distinguish our holistic approach to the product-pushing approach, the brokerage sells something and will call you six months from now when the next product comes. This is the perception amongst the consumers trying to make that distinction. I have to overcome that.

Q. Do you feel that the designation CFP has any recognition whatsoever with any of your clients?

A. No, and that's not right. It should have a much greater meaning. It should have the same impact as me telling clients I am a lawyer, which has enormous impact with my clients and prospective clients alike.

Q. Having gone through a CFP and having passed the bar, do you genuinely believe they are equivalent in their complexity with obvious alignment to the industries they serve?

A. Yes. They are two obviously very different exams and they are testing in two different ways. I certainly think that the CFP exam is extremely rigorous and should be that way so that anybody who is interested in becoming a CFP can't just study for 10 minutes and pass in 20 minutes. So they have to demonstrate the commitment up front that they are going to put their energy, time, and effort into it to get it, which to me shows they are interested in obtaining the license. The time commitment up front is important, again along the lines of someone making the commitment to take the six modules, pass six different exams, and then still study for the main exam. So to that point, it should have much greater impact to consumers if you are a CFP.

> *"If I knew then what I know now, it would have been, 'Are you kidding me? How the heck do you do that?'"*

Q. If you are with a new client, a younger client, what is the most important piece of advice you can give them?

A. For a new investor? Save as much as they possibly can in their 401K, with a dollar cost average outside of their 401K. It's not a sprint; it's a marathon. Get started early.

Q. Do you have minimums? Do you deal with a lot of younger people or not?

A. No. We deal with younger people, but they are not new investors and they are not new to planning, although some of them technically are because as you can appreciate, even some of the most "sophisticated" people have done no planning. But they have the means and the wherewithal, they have thought through planning, it's just not done as well as possible. We typically take on only five to ten new clients per year. We have probably maybe a hundred clients between the three of us.

Q. What do you see as the greatest challenge facing the industry?

A. The uncertainty of what the government is going to do next, and whether it's regulation of us, where taxes are going, where are the estate taxes going…basically where are they going with everything. I think uncertainty is the single greatest risk out there.

Q. What frustrates you most about the industry currently?

A. The government regulation as it currently is, and I think the perception that most consumers have of financial advisors is not a good one. Our challenge as holistic advisors is to differentiate ourselves by looking to develop a holistic approach and relationship based advisory capacity as opposed to product selling and product pushing. So maybe the best way to say it is the commoditization of financial advising.

Q. If you had to pick on one aspect of the current regulatory environment that you feel you would want to change, what would it be?

A. The uncertainty of it all. We are eternal optimists by nature, so we look at it as an opportunity. We look at the glass not ½ full, but ¾ full and say, "Well, the fact that people are talking about these things is a wonderful opportunity for us." When everything is hunky-dory and you are making 15% on your portfolio and you know exactly where things are going to be a year from now, why would you need a planner anyways? The fact is that because there is so much uncertainty, it makes it a wonderful opportunity. So even though it's frustrating and a great challenge in the negative sense, it's also a great challenge in the positive way and a frustration I would turn positive.

Q. If you were with a college grad that had a general degree in finance, and they were asking career advice of you, what would you tell them?

A. Be patient, talk to as many people as possible, don't spend a lot of money, and pick up the phone.

Q. When you look at the industry from a product standpoint, do you feel that it is overly complicated and unnecessarily burdened with product?

A. Yes, and as soon as you think you know the products, they change two months from now.

Q. So, taking a snapshot of the last three years, how significant has this period been if you were a new investor, a 45-year old in the middle of a career, or a 60-year old looking to retire?

A. Well, I look at it this way: in all three of these instances, if none of them had done any planning, all three of them were screwed. If all three of them did planning, they would be fine on paper, but mentally and emotionally the retiree would be a lot more emotional than the other two. I firmly believe that if all three had done some thorough planning, and put together a course to chart their next 5, 10, 15, 20 years, this period – looking back 15 or 20 years from now – will be a simple blip in the radar screen.

Q. So within the planning you do, are you managing money directly or are you running it through third-party managers?
A. Third-party money managers, using modern portfolio theory and a combination of actives and passives.

Q. Did you see a significant shift in your manager's approach in the last three years, or did they feel that they pretty much had the situation covered with the products and portfolios they were managing?
A. I haven't seen a dramatic shift. I have certainly seen some of the providers offer more products to try and capture the "Nervous Nelly's" of the world that want to be in the market and can't afford to be in a 1% bond account.

Q. What does your average week look like?
A. I want to preface what I am about to say: I take the approach that because I have the freedom, because I have the flexibility, because I have the independence, I am in control of my schedule. I have hired staff specifically to help me make sure that I stick to that schedule. I am firm when I hold to my schedule; so I believe that one of my main responsibilities to myself, my family, and to my clients, is to maintain a structured calendar. To help with my typical day, my BlackBerry is set up to turn on automatically at 7:30 in the morning, and it turns off at 7:00 at night. So although in modern technology world I am always accessible, the expectation with staff and with clients is that I am just like you; I work similar hours as you do. We structure our schedule so that Mondays and Fridays are generally office busy work days, meeting with staff, organizing for the current week, preparing what is going to happen for the following week, and debriefing for what happened during the previous week. Tuesdays, Wednesdays, and Thursdays tend to be reserved for meeting with clients. Every single Thursday, all three of us have it booked in our schedule to have an appointment day for new prospects and

appointments with clients to make sure the following week is as busy as it should be. So, with that being said, 40 or 50 hours a week? But because we are business owners, we are always in tune with what is going on. Our minds tend to always be on work and business and what we are supposed to be doing, but we are not at the desk on the phones for 90 hours a week, that's for sure.

Q. As a firm, what do you consider your most successful marketing strategy?
A. Without question, personal introductions from existing clients and referrals from other centers of influence or advisors.

Q. How tough were your first three years?
A. Well I started out the first two years on my own with my father who was in an investment only firm, with the eye towards no overhead, no glamorous expectations of trying to make a fortune or do anything huge; it was just getting out there talking to people and getting to know as many as possible. It wasn't my objective to go out and sell the next greatest and latest product. It was just to go out and develop relationships with people. So it was difficult, but I didn't know what I was getting myself into so I didn't have any baseline to compare at the time. If I knew then what I know now, it would have been, "Are you kidding me? How the heck do you do that?"

Q. How do you qualify retirement for yourself?
A. I don't think that is ever going to happen. I mean, retirement is maybe a change of career, but I don't see myself retiring. It's not my personality. I will be looking for the next challenge. If it relates to this business, it might be something very similar to what my senior partner is now doing where he's got two other people working with him or for him; however you want to define it. It would be nice knowing that somebody is minding the shop so that if my kid is married and having a

kid and they live in California, I can hop on a plane and head out there and not have to be concerned about who is taking care of the shop.

Q. If you had the chance to meet with Mr. Madoff, what would you want to say to him or ask him?
A. How the hell did he do it? I mean, most people who commit these schemes, the amount of time that they have to put into to developing the schemes, I've got to believe you could spend so much less time doing it legally.

Q. If there was one thing you could change, what would it be?
A. This goes to the point we were talking about before, to have a higher burden or more requirements in order to call one a financial planner. That would do the consumer a lot of good so that they could have a better idea of who they are suppose to trust. It would weed out more of the bad apples in the industry. There are a heck of a lot more good apples as opposed to bad apples, and the media obviously enjoys the one bad apple out of the thousand that are good apples. With the era of uncertainty that we are in, and the complexity of the subject matter, that would be my one change I would make.

I thought about this question quite a bit thinking, "Well geeze, if they raise the financial industry to a fiduciary standard of care, I am not quite sure if I am ready to say that's where we should go." Like I said before, it brings more potential litigation and more risk to us as advisors. So it would be somewhere in between where we are at now, and where the CFP board wants to go with raising the profession to a fiduciary standard.

Acknowledgements

I never imagined the effort and energy needed to create this book. Without the selfless participation by all the interviewees it would not have been possible. They provided their time but also their insights to an industry that is heavily regulated, competitive and easy to get lost in. They shared their experiences and the secrets to their individual success without hesitation or limitation. Their generosity has been extraordinary and I thank them each for helping in this endeavor.

To my wife and kids who have suffered my late evening editing sessions and supported me through the process, with their usual humor. My own colleagues and clients who have supported the idea and recognized the value in the information being accumulated and presented in one place.

About The Author

Financial Advisory was the furthest thing from my mind when I left school, I, like 3 generations before me followed a career in engineering. 25 years later I had motivation and reason to choose a second career and the good fortune to have the opportunity to join an established independent financial advisor.

As my exposure and experience with clients, the markets, brokers, wholesalers and compliance gained depth it struck me that the term Financial Planner is often misused, under appreciated and by some mis-represented. Many of the first generation of planners are now into their 50s and are looking to retire, planners in the midst of their careers are frustrated and there is severe lack of new planners coming to the industry; In large part due to the obscure barriers to entry, selling is by far the measurement of success not financial acumen. The industry as a whole has come under immense scrutiny [due to the activities of the few] and will be subject to further regulation and legislation. Clients often lack trust, planners are seen as glorified pitch men and the news seems to center on bad people doing bad things to good people. So why do people choose to be planners and what makes them successful? Where do the best planners gain the edge over the average planners? What characteristics link the good guys and what should a graduate looking for a career be aware of ? Equally – why should we as a general public use a planner? What should we look for and how do we choose the right planner for our personal situation?

To answer these and other questions I began talking to planners with differing degrees of industry experience and roles within it. Some are registered investment advisors and provide only advise, others offer products and make their livings from the commissions they gain from the sale of their products. Each discipline has its place and brings great value to those who seek assistance with their financial goals.

Financial planning is a noble occupation, often maligned unfairly. Average Americans need an advisor in the same manner they may need a doctor, it pays to have a check up once in a while so you can plan rather than react to bad and unexpected news.

My personal experiences have been very positive when dealing with clients of all types and I urge anyone who desires a career as a planner to persevere in the pursuit of their clients best interests, only good things can follow.

Visit our webpage below for details on when volume 2 will be published and join our growing community of readers:

http://financialplanners.50interviews.com

About 50 Interviews

50 Interviews is a publisher of books, CDs, videos, and software that serve to inform, educate, and inspire others on a wide range of topics. Timely insight, inspiration, collective wisdom, and best practices derived directly from those who have already succeeded. Authors surround themselves with those they admire, gain clarity of purpose, adopt critical beliefs, and build a network of peers to ensure success in that endeavor. Readers gain knowledge and perspective from those who have already achieved a result they desire.

Imagine a university where not only does each student get a textbook custom tailored to a curriculum they personally designed, but where each student literally becomes the author!

The mission of 50 Interviews is to provide aspiring, passionate, driven people a framework to achieve their dreams of becoming that which they aspire to be. Learning what it takes to be the best in your field; directly from those who have already succeeded. The ideal author is someone who desires to be a recognized expert in their field. You will be part of a community of authors who share your passion and who have learned firsthand how the *50 Interviews* concept works. A form of extreme education, the process promises to transform you into that which you aspire to become.

If you are interested in learning more, I would love to hear from you! You can contact me via email at: brian@50interviews.com, by phone: 970-215-1078 (Colorado), or through our website:

www.50interviews.com

All my best,
Brian Schwartz
Creator of *50 Interviews*

Other Titles

Additional topics based on the *50 Interviews* model that have already been released or are in development:

Athletes Over 50
by Don McGrath, Ph.D.

Young Entrepreneurs
by Nick Tart

Attraction Marketers
by Rob Christensen

Scientists
by David Giltner, Ph.D.

Physicians in Transition
by Rich Fernandez, MD

Property Managers
by Michael Levy

Professional Speakers
by Laura Lee Carter and Brian Schwartz

Attraction Marketers
by Rob Christensen

Video Marketers
by Randy Berry

Spiritualists
by Tuula Fai

Actors
by Ashley Pontius

Entrepreneurs
by Brian Schwartz

Successful Franchises
by Leslie Lautzenhiser

And many more...

Tap into more collective wisdom at:
www.50interviews.com

www.ingramcontent.com/pod-product-compliance
Lightning Source LLC
Chambersburg PA
CBHW052020070526
44584CB00016B/1831